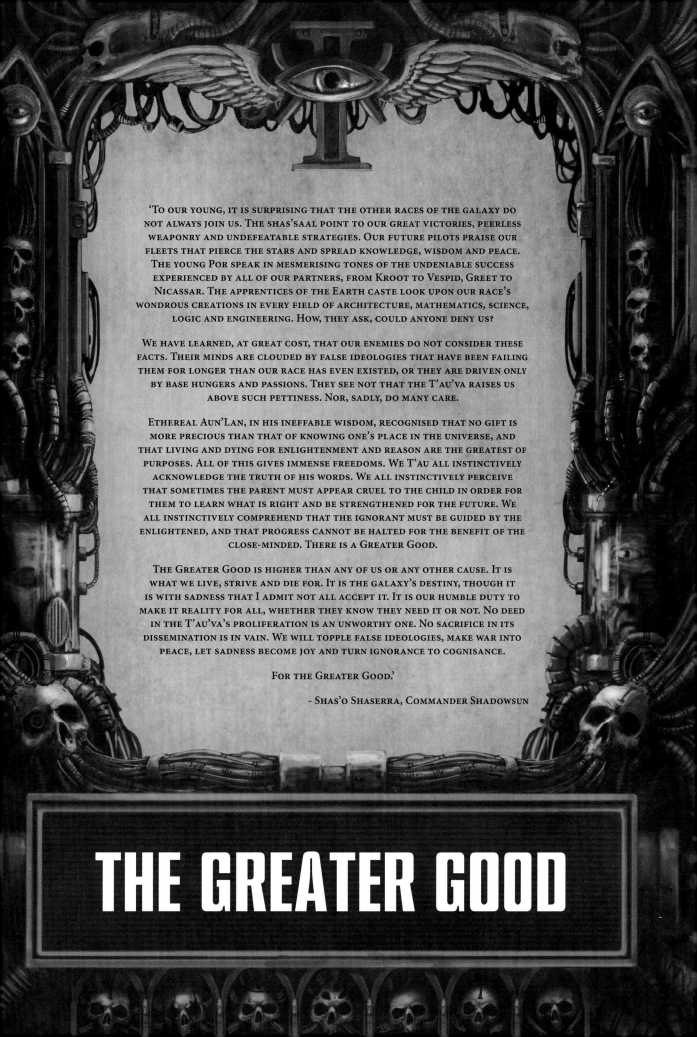

'To our young, it is surprising that the other races of the galaxy do not always join us. The shas'saal point to our great victories, peerless weaponry and undefeatable strategies. Our future pilots praise our fleets that pierce the stars and spread knowledge, wisdom and peace. The young Por speak in mesmerising tones of the undeniable success experienced by all of our partners, from Kroot to Vespid, Greet to Nicassar. The apprentices of the Earth caste look upon our race's wondrous creations in every field of architecture, mathematics, science, logic and engineering. How, they ask, could anyone deny us?

We have learned, at great cost, that our enemies do not consider these facts. Their minds are clouded by false ideologies that have been failing them for longer than our race has even existed, or they are driven only by base hungers and passions. They see not that the T'au'va raises us above such pettiness. Nor, sadly, do many care.

Ethereal Aun'Lan, in his ineffable wisdom, recognised that no gift is more precious than that of knowing one's place in the universe, and that living and dying for enlightenment and reason are the greatest of purposes. All of this gives immense freedoms. We T'au all instinctively acknowledge the truth of his words. We all instinctively perceive that sometimes the parent must appear cruel to the child in order for them to learn what is right and be strengthened for the future. We all instinctively comprehend that the ignorant must be guided by the enlightened, and that progress cannot be halted for the benefit of the close-minded. There is a Greater Good.

The Greater Good is higher than any of us or any other cause. It is what we live, strive and die for. It is the galaxy's destiny, though it is with sadness that I admit not all accept it. It is our humble duty to make it reality for all, whether they know they need it or not. No deed in the T'au'va's proliferation is an unworthy one. No sacrifice in its dissemination is in vain. We will topple false ideologies, make war into peace, let sadness become joy and turn ignorance to cognisance.

For the Greater Good.'

- Shas'o Shaserra, Commander Shadowsun

THE GREATER GOOD

CONTENTS

PRODUCED BY THE WARHAMMER STUDIO

With thanks to the Mournival and the Infinity Circuit for their additional playtesting services

Games Workshop Ltd, Willow Rd, Lenton, Nottingham, NG7 2WS

games-workshop.com

INTRODUCTION

The T'au Empire's Fifth Sphere Expansion has begun in earnest. Reunited with the surviving heroes of the Fourth Sphere, the T'au work to fulfil their destiny and bring ever more worlds and peoples into the fold of the Greater Good. These populations may be ignorant of the greatness that could be theirs, but they will be taught.

Beset on many sides by dead space or formidable alien empires, many years ago the T'au sought to circumnavigate these obstacles in their quest to unite the galaxy under the Greater Good. They envisioned this Fourth Sphere Expansion as the greatest of its kind in their history, but it failed, apparently lost with all hands in a technological disaster. Only years later were survivors discovered, and Commander Shadowsun took leadership of the Fifth Sphere Expansion to reunite the T'au Empire with its lost kin. Powering through the Startide Nexus wormhole, Shadowsun's fleet emerged at the Nem'yar Atoll in a region known to the Imperium as the Chalnath Expanse. A period of intense colonisation culminated in a ferocious battle against the Death Guard, but the T'au secured victory, and they are now prepared to strike out again.

Humanity's beleaguered soldiery in the Chalnath Expanse stand against foe after foe even with their skies scarred by the Great Rift. Holding on to their faith in the Emperor with all their might, they fight to quell rebellions and uprisings as well as xenos invasion.

Even an armed force as insidious as the Genestealer Cults cannot count on their complex plans to unfold without difficulty. They are not alone in wanting domination over the planet they call home; other races and ideologies have designs upon it, not least the T'au and their Greater Good. The Genestealer Cults are tenacious and devious, and their claws are dug deep into the Chalnath Expanse. They will do what it takes to keep competitors away from their territory, spilling as much blood as possible to keep it for the Star Children.

IN THIS BOOK

This book is part of Psychic Awakening, an ongoing series set in the aftermath of the Great Rift. It contains an overview from the perspectives of the T'au Empire, the Genestealer Cults and the Astra Militarum.

Inside you will find:

- The unfolding drama of the conflict in the Chalnath Expanse and the T'au Empire's Fifth Sphere Expansion.
- A mission to echo the narrative of *The Greater Good*.
- Updated rules for the T'au Empire, Genestealer Cults and Astra Militarum, including datasheets, Relics, psychic powers, Stratagems and more.
- Rules on how to create your own T'au Sept, Genestealer Cult Creed or Astra Militarum Regiment.

THE FIFTH SPHERE EXPANSION

When a returning recon probe proved that some of the Fourth Sphere T'au still lived, the Fifth Sphere Expansion was founded to reunite the survivors with the empire. Beyond the Startide Nexus they met with strange findings and foul foes.

Barely a quarter of the Fourth Sphere fleet had escaped the hellish sub-realm they had been pitched into by the mass failure of their ships' AL-38 Slipstream modules. Countless colonists were slain by murderous and sadistic creatures dwelling there that defied all T'au understanding of the universe. Given the horror they had endured, most of the survivors could barely speak of how they escaped. It surprised many of the Fifth Sphere T'au that what discomforted their lost kin more than anything else was the presence of non-T'au species in the Fifth Sphere fleet. The Fourth Sphere's own auxiliaries could not be found, with only dark theories circulating as to why.

Despite the many questions that still hung ominously in the air, Shadowsun wasted little time in progressing the Fifth Sphere Expansion. The Nem'yar Atoll was wild and contested by myriad races. Piratical Ork fleets terrorised the Ful'na Nebulae in the east, and scattered Tyranid tendrils roamed hungrily. Several Imperial worlds were swept up quickly by Shadowsun's forces, having been left vulnerable and isolated by the Devourer of Hope – known to Humans as the Great Rift. The Fourth Sphere T'au relished war against these Humans, carrying out acts of incredible barbarity such as the Slaughter at Sal'kyo, the Fi'liol Station Bloodshed and many others that haunted Shadowsun and the Ethereal High Council. Such were these atrocities that many commanders of the Fourth Sphere were subjected to the ritual punishment of Malk'la. Despite these hindrances, a multitude of colonies were established.

Only months after the miraculous reunification with the Fourth Sphere survivors, the Nem'yar Atoll came under attack. Without warning an immense armada of ships resembling hideously changed Imperial vessels broke into realspace before the Startide Nexus itself, disgorging torrents of ordnance and boarding torpedoes. The Nexus' defence platforms were buffeted by shot that corroded their crisp armoured hulls in the blink of an eye. Boarded defenders found themselves under attack from enemies that resembled Space Marines, but with bodies grotesquely degenerated and beset by foul plagues. Many wielded huge scythes that could cut a Crisis Battlesuit in twain, or carried weapons that spewed gouts of toxic slime. Despite their hideous deformities they were terrifyingly resilient, shrugging off withering weapons fire with impunity.

For all the surprise of the attack, the T'au forces were highly disciplined and

the defence fleets responded with laudable speed. A great many of the invading ships were destroyed in salvoes of heavy fire, but they were remarkably durable, like the hulking abominations that crewed them, and large numbers more survived. They disgorged thousands of warriors from their heaving bulks who descended upon stellar fortifications and ships with incredible ferocity, spreading their filth with joyous abandon. Broken reports spoke of the T'au themselves being infected by the invaders' disgusting contagions. None could explain how the T'au could be affected by gue'la diseases, and yet they were. Some orbital stations were so ravaged that their captains' last acts before succumbing to illness were to set their stations to self-destruct, lest what they suffered spread to others.

When Shadowsun learned of the assault she responded without hesitation. Correlating data from battles on Kellik and Calendhula, Shadowsun identified the attackers as the Death Guard. The Nexus could not fall to these monsters. The Death Guard could not be allowed to enter it and attack the main T'au Empire.

Upon arrival at the Nexus, Shadowsun's fleet broke down into small battle groups, each with dedicated targets and responsibilities. Some relieved beleaguered defence stations, while others engaged the Death Guard fleet head on. Every action was part of detailed, overlapping plans to present so many targets to the Death Guard that their fleet would fracture. Battle groups taunted and baited, retreating then striking again. So this continued, but the casualties mounted at an enormous rate. Though the number of putrid Death Guard wrecks began to grow, it was not enough to stop them. Scores of vessels still made to enter the Nexus.

In a rare moment of doubt, Shadowsun considered that it might not be possible to win and ordered for the empire to be warned. In a blaze of light, an advanced prototype messenger drone sped from Shadowsun's command ship, past the Death Guard fleet and into the Startide Nexus.

As some of the Death Guard ships burrowed into the Nexus, those left behind suddenly withdrew from battle, their pestilential hulls absorbing terrific punishment as they made for a warp jump point. Vengeful T'au destroyed some, but a great many escaped, peeling away from the fields of foetid wrecks like a bandage drawn back from a still-seeping wound.

On the other side of the Nexus, in the Zone of Silence, the Startide defence fleets waited with baited breath. Reinforcements had been pulled in from across the empire following the warning carried by the drone.

But nothing happened. No foul plague-ship emerged from the Nexus. For months the T'au operated at the highest level of readiness, but there was nothing. The waiting was almost worse than battle, such was the tension. At any point horrific forces could appear and submerge the Zone of Silence in a deluge of virulence. To what end the Death Guard's destructive attack had been launched, theories abounded. T'au strategists had no way of knowing whether this end had even been achieved, but all agreed the threat persisted. The Nexus' permanent defences were increased, and battlefield data was scrutinised for answers.

THE CHALNATH EXPANSE

The Chalnath Expanse, home to the Nem'yar Atoll, was riven by conflict. T'au fleets discovered Imperial worlds in the grip of civil war and mass civilian uprisings. Bringing the systems of this region into the Greater Good would require immense resolve and discipline. Shadowsun was confident that her warriors were capable.

The Humans of the Chalnath Expanse had been beset by disaster after disaster. Firstly the emergence of the Great Rift, accompanied by T'au overtures and invasions, and secondly the Genestealer Cult uprisings. Instances of mutation and seditious witchery increased, and Governors and ruling councils bickered over which of these blights were causes and which were symptoms as they fought to retain control.

Not one system avoided conflict. Shadowsun herself attacked Astorgius in the Thaxaril System. Though the Ctesiphus and Arrajian Systems were not directly assaulted by T'au forces, they were subject to Genestealer Cult uprisings so successful that more than half of their key worlds fell in a matter of months. Those few that remained loyal held on by a thread, their enduring faith in the Emperor all that gave them strength. The defenders of Haephos were embroiled in an intense guerrilla war with xenos cultists, complicated by murderous T'au infiltrators and their duplicitous diplomats. The Riatov System became an inferno of bloodshed between the T'au, Astra Militarum and Genestealer Cultists. The inhabitants of Vorotheion in the Barolyr System counted themselves fortunate for some time, before cursing their luck when the first forays of T'au encroachment triggered a mass uprising from long forgotten parts of the underhive in their capital.

The T'au's core strategy remained the same as with any sphere of expansion. Disenfranchised Human populations were wooed with tales of the wonders of the Greater Good. Insurrectionist cells were cultivated and ambitious leaders supported. Still, the T'au never expected to contend with the Genestealer Cults. When battlefield data was accumulated and autopsies were carried out on the corpses of strangely mutated Humans, the horrible truth was revealed. They discovered monstrous hybrids of Human and Tyranid genetic strands. Debate raged amongst the Earth caste as to how this was possible, but all agreed that these creatures had to be destroyed with extreme prejudice.

The T'au were quick to take advantage of the pandemonium of the wars already raging between Imperial forces and the Genestealer Cults, but it was not just the presence of Human-Tyranid hybrids that surprised them. Gue'vesa auxiliaries talked of 'miracles' that often occurred around the Imperium's priest caste, defying any scientific understanding. The reports told of strange anomalies of Human behaviour; sometimes outbursts of violent insanity even occurred amongst the gue'vesa themselves.

Meanwhile, strange portents were seen by the Chalnath Expanse's Genestealer Cults. Many expected the arrival of the Star Children to be heralded by a great veil of shadow and silence, according to their scriptures and founding legends. When their leaders observed an increase in Human psychic potential on their worlds, and a rising number of their own Maguses being born, they were concerned. For many these omens meant one thing – the Star Children deemed them unworthy, and they would have to fight all the harder for their deities' attention and blessings.

With the Imperials clinging harder to their own oppressive faith, and the T'au invaders' false creed of the Greater Good capturing the minds of countless Humans, many Genestealer Cults rose up in the name of the Star Children they so revered and worshipped. They would assert the strength of their deities and, in doing so, prove their own worthiness. Some even saw the increased number of Maguses as a positive sign, a weapon given to them by the Star Children to destroy their enemies.

In the eyes of the Imperium, the xenos threatened the very souls of the people. The great cathedra of the Ministorum sent out their priests far and wide, believing that only unshakeable faith could see Mankind through this most severe of tests. The knowledge that the Emperor protects reassured all, from the lowliest factory menial to the greatest planetary lord. The Emperor had seen them safe for thousands of years through great trials and turbulent times, and he would see them safe through this too – or so the gilded vox-horns in every hab-block, manufactorum and basilica blared.

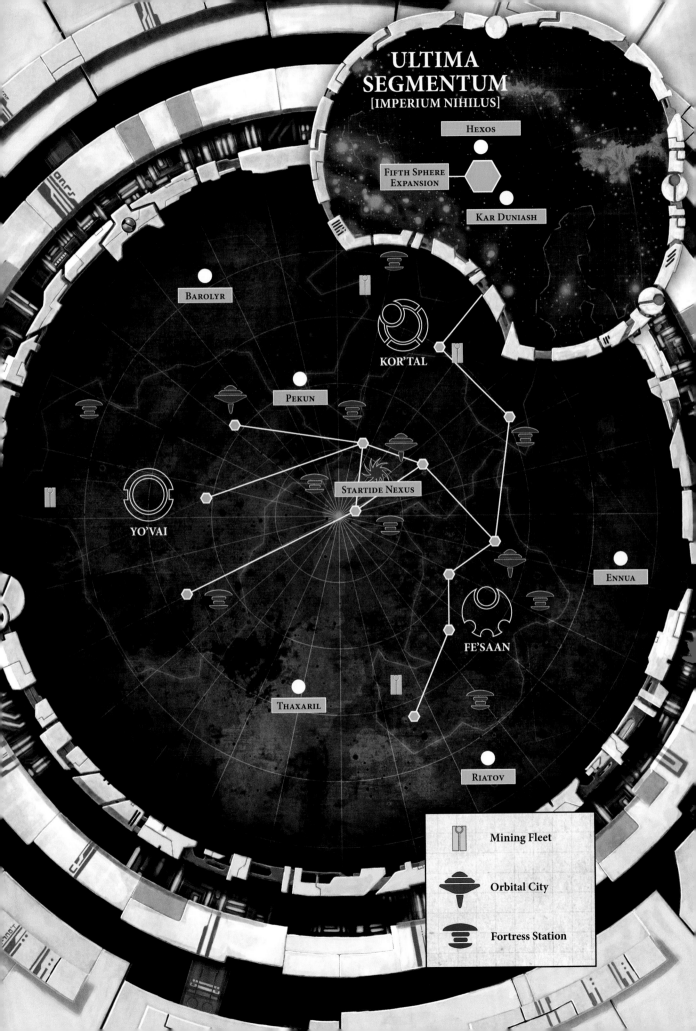

ULTIMA SEGMENTUM
[IMPERIUM NIHILUS]

HEXOS

FIFTH SPHERE
EXPANSION

KAR DUNIASH

BAROLYR

KOR'TAL

PEKUN

STARTIDE NEXUS

YO'VAI

ENNUA

FE'SAAN

THAXARIL

RIATOV

	Mining Fleet
	Orbital City
	Fortress Station

THE RAZING OF ASTORGIUS

The Imperial cardinal world of Astorgius was celebrated across the sector for its magnificent architecture, incredible wealth and priceless relics. When the planet's unshakeable devotion to the Emperor saw its leaders reject the T'au's overtures without hesitation, Commander Shadowsun herself led the resulting assault.

The severed heads of the T'au delegation were sent to meet Astorgius' leadership, presented to Shadowsun in five large, gilded chests lined with plush red velvet – one for each caste. The Humans had shown that they knew the difference between the castes, that they had listened to the T'au delegates and murderously rejected them all the same. The death of the Ethereal in particular made Shadowsun's blood boil. She resolved that an example must be made of these gue'la. Such an act would surely bring others into the fold of the T'au'va more peaceably.

Shadowsun took solace in the fact that countless more 'diplomatic' efforts were being made all over Kesh'val – the T'au's name for Astorgius. Hundreds of Water caste agents met in secret with middle-ranking laymen across the planet. They learned that the united front presented by Astorgius' governing body was in fact a thin veneer that concealed the world's highly fractious politics. Every family had aspirations, fears, rivals and enemies – all exploitable by the T'au. In some places the T'au formed agreements, promising positions of influence after the planet's fall in exchange for alliance. In others, T'au troops trained in clandestine warfare launched raids against specific targets, their goal to make their attacks resemble those of rival factions. Insurrectionists were encouraged and armed. Intelligence was gathered, constantly feeding data into Shadowsun's growing picture of the future battlescape.

Some reports were more disturbing and unexpected. Deep in crypts, tunnels and other hidden areas, T'au reconnaissance elements found strange graffiti depicting worms or serpents. Some even recorded sightings of multi-limbed creatures scurrying away into the darkness. At this stage none could say with certainty what these beings were, though the T'au were aware that weaknesses in Human genetics sometimes led to ugly mutations and freak births.

In keeping with her mastery of Kauyon – the art of the patient hunter – Shadowsun did not launch her assault on Astorgius for months. She knew that the more undermined and fractured the planet's leadership was, the swifter her campaign would be overall. By

the time T'au dropships launched in their thousands, Astorgius was on the brink of civil war. Such were Shadowsun's preparations that not even alien conquest was threat enough to bring Astorgius' conflicting factions together. Nonetheless, those intending to resist readied themselves. All over Astorgius, the vast cathedra-cities that made up the bulk of its inhabited areas revealed their capabilities. Gilded domes opened like blossoming flowers to reveal banks of anti-air cannons. Panes of stained glass windows hundreds of metres long slid into their frames to unveil huge hangar bays filled with swift fighter craft. Processions of robe-clad monks took to the streets and barracks, whipping up crowds of people and ranks of soldiers into frenzies of hatred for the alien.

The T'au made no direct assaults against these formidable defences, seeing such a strategy as a waste of lives and resources. Instead, their warriors were deployed in those urban districts deemed friendly following the Water caste campaigns, or in the vast open spaces that were maintained as pleasure gardens, game parks or simply left wild. Nevertheless, the T'au contingents moved into battle swiftly, determined to bring the fighting for Kesh'val to a swift conclusion. Armoured Interdiction Cadres duelled Astra Militarum Armoured Companies in the Sajitaryan Fields, Hammerheads picking off Leman Russ battle tanks with their devastating railguns. The urban sprawl of Belenok was stalked by roving tribes of Kroot working in tandem with Breacher Cadres, their task to root out hunkered down Human infantry that had created a veritable fortress of razor wire, weapon pits and bunkers. Kroot Carnivores used their keen hunting senses to discover well-concealed gue'la soldiers, while Breacher Teams employed their advanced close-quarters training to destroy Human positions with their pulse blasters.

Battles played out across the world as the T'au kept up a constant stream of hit-and-run attacks. Shadowsun desired to demonstrate the T'au's military superiority by defeating as many of the fanatical enemy as possible, to force surrender without giving the Imperium anything like a solid victory of its own.

But that surrender never came. Human resistance was dogged, their belief in their Emperor especially strong. Shadowsun was particularly troubled by accounts of 'miracles', as the gue'vesa and Human prisoners described them. Some told of blinding light that obscured the charges of hundreds of Human troops before they smashed into Fire Warrior lines; others were barely credible tales of priest-types flying through the air with vicious chainblades to carve through battlesuits in mid-flight. Whatever the reports, none conformed to the physical laws as the T'au understood them, yet drone-recorded battle footage showed such events occurring. So persuasive were some of these events that elements of the gue'vesa turned on their T'au allies, screaming their repentance as they opened fire on those they had called comrades only minutes before.

Frequent breakouts of insanity occurred in the T'au ranks, of the same kind the T'au had encountered after the Devourer of Hope emerged. As before, these were confined to Humans and other non-T'au species, and were swiftly concealed by the T'au hierarchy. Any T'au discovered referring to strange aliens stepping out of the ruined corpses of insane Humans were quarantined and dispatched to special hospitals for recovery. When a detachment of Fourth Sphere T'au was discovered by their Fifth Sphere allies killing prisoners, including Humans who had already embraced the Greater Good, its

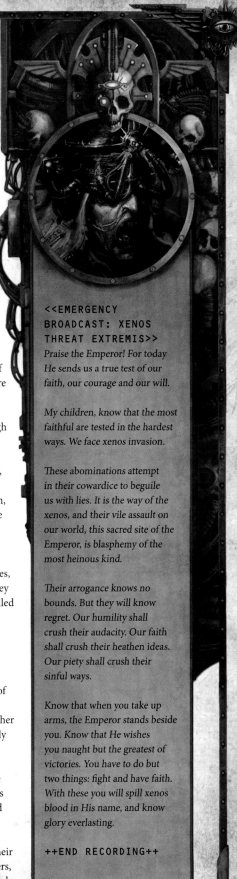

commander stated that one day the rest of the empire would thank him, before he took the Malk'la.

As the fighting raged on all over Astorgius, Shadowsun looked keenly for a crucial weakness that she could capitalise on to bring the bloody war to an end. The Humans' morale was strong, stronger than she had ever seen elsewhere. They held to their beliefs with a vigour that almost defied imagination. Their faith was their life. It was their greatest strength. Could that make it their greatest weakness?

Gathered intelligence indicated that the Humans fought hard over sites and artefacts of particular religious significance, and that if these fell or were captured, acts of individual surrender spiked. When Human propaganda boasted that not a single cathedra-city had fallen, Shadowsun knew her next move. She would topple the planet's greatest cathedra-city, Iglesor Magna. The capture of such a place would surely cripple the resolve of the staunchest Human defenders. They would know their Emperor was not with them when the broadcasts filled with T'au declarations of victory, and peace offerings to those Humans that still resisted, began in earnest.

Shadowsun's forces made to surround Iglesor Magna. Potential Human relief forces were subject to relentless assault as Riptide and Ghostkeel Battlesuits ambushed armoured columns and innumerable swarms of drones were deployed to harass infantry forces. T'au contingents surrounding the cathedra-city were under strict orders from Shadowsun to leave clear a passage outwards – she could not risk the defenders believing that they had no option but a fight to the death. Escape had to be seen as a real possibility for them, although Shadowsun's forces were secretly placed to kill or capture any that actually attempted to break out.

The T'au intercepted and hacked all Human communications, and broadcast demands to surrender. Those that handed themselves over, they declared, would be offered food, water and safety. Not one gue'la capitulated.

Advanced Infiltration Cadres made the first forays into Iglesor Magna, striking from all directions. They expected fierce resistance from the outset, their only mission to identify defensive emplacements and mark them out for destruction. However, they were actually able to advance several kilometres into the city, past abandoned defensive cannons and bunkers. They did not know why the gue'la had yielded these positions, and Shadowsun cautiously ordered her follow-up contingents to begin securing them so that they could not be reoccupied by the Humans. Hundreds of Fire Warrior teams tactically advanced from gilded column to gilded column, through small chapels, accommodation for menials and enormous basilicas large enough to house dozens of armoured vehicles.

Shadowsun believed that the absence of defenders could only mean a trap, so the advance cadres were ordered to take deliberate care. In spite of herself, Shadowsun looked forward to the Humans' efforts to attack her well-trained warriors, and to seeing them fail. But

she underestimated her opposition. Hundreds of unsuspecting Fire Warriors were killed when parts of ceiling frescoes were peeled away to reveal murder holes through which the defenders dropped explosives and grenades. Trapdoors large enough to swallow Stormsurges opened beneath the advancing T'au forces. Those unfortunate enough to fall through were butchered by zealots, or destroyed by the autocannons and lascannons of waiting heavy weapons teams.

So began months of guerrilla war and counter-insurgency actions. Kauyon and Mont'ka strategies were carried out at squad level. The Humans knew every secret passage of their cathedra-city, using them to their immense advantage and in so doing claiming countless T'au lives. The T'au drew the defenders into ambushes and kill zones of their own, utilising the secret passageway network themselves where they discovered it, or deliberately threatening certain artefacts or shrines to draw out Iglesor Magna's robed defenders. As casualties mounted, Shadowsun refused to overcommit her forces in all-out assault. To do so would be to throw away lives, and as the noose of T'au forces tightened around the defenders, surrender seemed inevitable. But no surrender came.

Shadowsun also had to withdraw her gue'vesa forces, whose brutality towards the defenders had grown to heights she could not tolerate. Torture of prisoners and mutilation of the dead were common. Some gue'vesa openly wore jewellery made from the extracted teeth of dead Astorgians. They frequently disobeyed orders to hold position, instead pursuing retreating foes, making themselves and others vulnerable in the process. Strange anomalies and insanity outbreaks became more frequent where Humans fought other Humans.

Despite all this, the T'au were winning. More territory was

secured with each passing day as the defenders' numbers depleted and their supplies ran low. The desperation of Shadowsun's enemies was finally revealed when thousands of them launched an overwhelming attack to break out. They were nearly successful, such was the surprise they achieved. Thundering companies of battle tanks and tens of thousands of zealous troops came perilously close to overrunning the city's western districts. It was only thanks to T'au discipline and the careful deployment of Rapid Response Cadres full of Crisis Battlesuits and Devilfish-mounted Fire Warrior teams that the attack was stymied. The failure of this assault broke the defenders' backs, such were the resources required to launch it, and finally pockets of emaciated and terrified Humans began to surrender. The pace of the T'au's advance soon quickened and the noose tightened completely. Shadowsun herself took to the field in the final battles of the conflict, as the last of Iglesor Magna's starving Humans surrendered or were cut down, her twin fusion blasters incinerating countless defenders and melting through scores of bunkers.

Shadowsun's victory at Iglesor Magna was projected all over Kesh'val, the glory of the T'au'va shown for all to see. The Ethereals of the Fifth Sphere smiled, knowing that surely this spelled the end of Human resistance on the planet. Water caste aides prepared victory speeches, but the move was premature.

Seeing the mighty spires of Iglesor Magna topple to the ground and shatter into millions of pieces had simply stiffened the resolve of those who still fought. With sadness, Shadowsun had little choice but to accept that much blood was still to be spilled, though Humanity's suicidal drive to fight regardless of casualties made her shudder.

After the battle's conclusion, Commander Shadowsun walked the wards of Hospital Ship 227. So many of these vessels had been constructed since the Damocles Crusade that the T'au had ceased naming them. Shadowsun had come unannounced, dressed in simple robes. Bunk after bunk was filled with wounded and dying T'au. Many had lost limbs, while others were held down with tight restraints, driven mad by horror. Earth caste orderlies rushed past bearing medicines and surgical equipment, so busy that they failed to notice that Shadowsun herself walked amongst them. Each hospital ship had capacity for

around five thousand wounded. Every one of the dozens in Astorgius' orbit were operating well beyond those limits. Shadowsun saw the dead jettisoned from airlocks in their hundreds. They would normally have been burned in honourable funeral ceremonies, but such were their numbers and the demand for space that there was simply no time to observe tradition. The Commander knew that not one of the fallen would begrudge this necessity; none of it mattered so long as it was done for the Greater Good. Battle still raged on Astorgius, and Shadowsun would not let their sacrifice be in vain.

THE HAEPHOS CONTAINMENT

Haephos was in the grip of rebellion. The Great Rift had brought panic and fear, its ominous presence in the skies shattering the population's sense of safety. All contact with the wider Imperium was lost, though the planet's governor, Zula Hatiar, had no reason to believe she would not continue to meet her tithe requirements.

<<Fifth Sphere
Expansion Campaign
Log, rotaa 257>>

We cannot fail. We represent the hope of our people; indeed, the hope of the Greater Good. We are the tip of the spear, the pioneers. We have gone where no T'au thought possible.

We were on the brink of deadlock. Implacable, ignorant and predatory foes stood at every turn, but we were true to our cause. With the tenacity and audaciousness that characterises our race, we persevered.

Those of the Fourth Sphere were truly the bravest. What they must have endured... what risks they took... to then emerge alone in the galactic wilderness...

To maintain order, to build what would be our stepping stone into the wider Nem'yar Atoll – despite not knowing whether they would ever hear from their kin again – took immeasurable courage and conviction. This should be the envy of us all.

But they have been changed. The extent of their sacrifice and what it has done to them is difficult to contemplate, but I cannot condone their actions.

++END RECORDING++

Densely populated Haephos was a mining world in the Pekun System. A key planet in the region, it had produced vast quantities of promethium and metals for use in munitions for thousands of years. Like many Imperial worlds, its population had suffered terribly since the Great Rift's emergence. In their fright, many of Haephos' people had turned to firebrands and demagogues, whose powerful message of survival through change appeared to offer the security the Imperium could not.

Governor Hatiar's planetary defence regiments were faced with rapidly increasing outbreaks of mutation, and a multitude of cults devoted to what they called the 'One-eyed Liege'. One such cult, the Followers of the Red Monarch, were responsible for dozens of atrocities, most notoriously the Eusebya Tunnel Collapse which claimed over thirty thousand lives. Meanwhile, the Cyclopeans – a cult whose members were noted for ritually putting out one of their own eyes in honour of their deity – launched an attack on the Calixtos Spaceport, delaying promethium exports by several weeks.

Freak events described by eyewitnesses as heretical sorcery and witchcraft became more common. The Lascari Mine Massacre, the Muliga Refinery Inferno and the Insanity of Hab-block 27Λ were but a handful of instances in an ever growing list of malign events. When

the Black Ships of the Adeptus Astra Telepathica failed to arrive according to their schedule, Haephos was left with thousands of dangerous psykers in its custody. This was seen as an opportunity by the increasingly desperate governor, however. Against advice from her counsellors, Zula Hatiar offered freedom to some of the psykers in exchange for their help in seeking out mutants and rogue witches. Those that did not comply, willingly or otherwise, were culled.

The initial success of this campaign surprised even Governor Hatiar. With the psykers' aid, the Followers of the Red Monarch were hunted down and destroyed by four regiments of Haephosian Phalanxari in the dense hab-blocks of Zonora City's south-west district. The mutants of Titanium Shaft 67 were burned out by the Catachan 99th 'Land Sharks', and the 343rd 'Devil Hunters' were temporarily stationed on the planet to provide jungle warfare training for the Haephosian regiments. The undersea mines of the Anthemion Trench were the site of fierce fighting between the Cult of Chalkonides and more than thirty companies of the Haephosian Tritons. Renowned combat aquanauts, the Tritons restored the mines to full function in a matter of weeks, leaving no heretic alive.

Following the successes of her campaign up to that point, when a violently migrating mutant colony of hundreds of thousands was identified in the vast tunnel complexes beneath the Latinion sub-continent, Hatiar was convinced that victory was inevitable. Infantry from twenty Haephosian Phalanxari regiments were dispatched, alongside seven regiments of Haephosian Klibanarii replete with squadrons of thundering Leman Russ battle tanks, flame-belching Hellhounds and striding Sentinels. A dozen allied regiments from other worlds were also allocated to what was expected to be a glorious battle.

The braying mutants encountered by the combined Imperial forces were swiftly crushed, ground beneath armoured tracks or cut down by waves of accurate las and heavy bolter fire. Nests and homesteads were purged with gouts of burning promethium or virulent, flesh-melting toxins. However, soon the mutants' great numbers began to tell, and they pushed back. The sounds of battle filled tunnels of every kind, from those so narrow that guardsmen could only walk them single file, to those wide enough for a company of Leman Russ tanks to drive through abreast. Vox lines were flooded with the screams of guardsmen being shredded by savage creatures, or tank crews crying for aid as their vehicles were swamped with deluges of noxious vomit. The clashes reached their peak intensity in the junctions where various tunnels met, amongst abandoned way stations and checkpoints. It was here too that the nature of the war on Haephos changed completely, and Governor Hatiar learned just why the mutants fought with such unbridled savagery.

They were fleeing something else. Something worse than the Astra Militarum forces that came to destroy them. Others dwelled in Latinion's nightmarish underworld, and they too sought the destruction of the mutants so that they could claim the planet for themselves. These other cults had bided their time, growing their strength with a patience and diligence unmatched by the mutants the Haephosian forces had faced so far. The first Imperial troops to encounter this new threat identified weaponised mining vehicles and Achilles Ridgerunners advancing at speed, its humanoid crew unleashing torrents of ammunition from rapid-firing weapons as they ran down those too slow to escape them.

This unexpected foe attacked the Imperial forces immediately, catching them totally by surprise. Expecting a swift victory against an ill-disciplined enemy, Haephos' troops found themselves on the defensive against a highly organised and well-equipped force. Infantry platoons were encircled and outflanked by foes mounted on Atalan Jackals before being pounced

THE HAEPHOS CONTAINMENT

Haephosian efforts to cleanse the world of mutation and witchcraft stirred nascent Genestealer Cults hidden deep beyond the reach of the most ardent Imperial enforcer. Once discovered, the cults began their uprising all over Haephos, their key targets the planet's spaceports. The hammer of the Imperium responded in kind, committing vast military resources to the cults' destruction.

IMPERIUM

CLEANSING OF ELETYRIO

Haephosian Phalanxari	13 infantry regiments
Haephosian Klibanarii	3 armoured regiments
Haephosian Tritons	17 infantry companies
Catachan Jungle Fighters	2 infantry regiments
Thaxarillian Guard	3 infantry regiments
Yamnin Volunteers	4 artillery musters
Riatov Grenadiers	2 infantry regiments
Riatov Dragoons	2 armoured regiments
Dremian Carronademen	4 artillery regiments
Faeburn Bullgryn Auxilia	4 brute regiments

DEFENCE OF THE VOLUSHUN SHIPYARDS

Haephosian Phalanxari	6 infantry regiments
Haephosian Klibanarii	2 armoured regiments
Haephosian Tritons	27 infantry companies
Indigan Praefects	2 infantry regiments
16th Paruthan Immortals 'God-slayers'	1 super-heavy regiment
Krobos 22nd Ratling Sniper Auxilia & Catering Corps	1 regiment
Gnarvis Ogryn Auxilia	2 brute regiments
Formund Scorpions	2 artillery regiments

Addendum: Lists above partial, inclusive only of regular forces. Expanded and detailed in file 47.φЋ.52L. Subject to alteration.

GENESTEALER CULTS

SEIZURE OF THE URBIKAN MEGA-REFINERY

Urbikan Barrel-cleansing Guild 217	4 brood cycles
South West Pipe Network Delvers	3 brood cycles
The Wyrm Followers	1 sub-sect
Union of the Sacred Coils	6 claws
Heralds of the Star Children Eterna	2 brood cycles
Chemlurkers	9 claws
Claws of the Urbikan Wastedump	1 sub-sect
North East Quadrant Security Detachment 17	4 claws

CULL OF THE LATINION SUB-CONTINENT

The Daughters of Devotion	4 sub-sects
The Sons of Subservience	4 sub-sects
Way Station 4 Quality Control Board	9 claws
Denizens of the North Tunnel Grand Sewer Delta	11 brood cycles
Devoted Lineage	12 brood cycles
Fiends of Service Tunnel 64	6 claws
Offspring of the Great Star Worm	8 sub-sects
Holders of the Coiled Truth	10 brood cycles

Full analysis of Genestealer Cults forces impossible due to contradicting reports, unclear identification markers and unreliable vox intercepts and communications. Additional listings in file 962.βx.HN9. Treat with extreme caution. Foe duplicitous even by xenos standards. Total foe numbers estimated in tens of millions or greater.

on by clawed, multi-limbed horrors clad in well-worn mining gear. Sentinel squadrons were beset by heavily muscled monstrosities that ripped open cockpits and tore apart the pilots. Conflicting reports claimed that this new foe was made up of traitors, xenos or new strains of mutant.

Some Imperial officers were in a position to rally their troops in time and take some initiative. The 'Bastion Breakers' Leman Russ Demolisher company charged head-on into an onslaught of Goliath Rockgrinders. Such bravery cost the lives of all the tanks' crews, but stymied an assault that could have destroyed much of the 12th Riatov Grenadiers' 5th and 6th Companies. The 81st Haephosian Klibanarii's 2nd Hellhound Company raced at high speed to relieve trapped Pekuni Hearthguard, striking with such fury that not only were their allies rescued, but hundreds of cultists were incinerated by burning promethium. Some of these cultists were even successfully captured, though those that achieved this incredible feat were executed for unlawful contact with foes of the Imperium after their captives were taken away.

Within a matter of hours the battle was over – the new enemy had slunk away and retreated despite their significant battlefield advantages. The mutant colony had indeed been destroyed, but thousands of Imperial troops were also slain, their broken bodies scattered over multiple battlefields. Hundreds of tank wrecks burned, the smog poisoning the thin subterranean air. Governor Hatiar, denied her swift and magnificent victory, was shaken. Against all military advice she withdrew her surviving troops rather than ordering a pursuit, hoping that this new foe would never be encountered again. Her regiments had scared them off; they would surely not return.

But return they did. Simultaneous uprisings broke out across Haephos, each one with similar attributes – repurposed civilian vehicles loaded with weaponry, many-limbed monsters with claws and wicked blades and humanoid warriors clad in battered mining attire and wielding crude weapons. There was another common thread, in that all focused particular attention on the planet's spaceports, in particular Eletyrio, Haephos' largest. Hatiar had little idea what kind of intelligence drove these creatures, but even a fool could see that their actions were no coincidence. They sought to escape. Hatiar was determined that this would not happen, committing her generals to ensuring that the spaceports held. She could not risk the wider Imperium learning of what horrors her planet harboured, and had allowed to fester in its depths.

Eletyrio was the size of a city. Its bustling docks supported thousands of commercial and military spacecraft and heaved with servitors, crews going about vital on-shore business and mysterious agents of the Adeptus Mechanicus. Vast landing pads sat amid storehouses packed with supplies ready to be dispatched off-world. Colossal fuel tanks kept the engines of Imperial trade running. Hab-blocks for workers were everywhere, amongst workshops where machinery ceaselessly groaned, banged and clanked.

But the sounds of industry swiftly changed to sounds of battle. Alien chants and screeches met the battle oaths of Imperial priests and soldiery, and the air filled with the crack of lasguns, the roar of cannons and the chug of repeating guns. A place of commerce and civility had become one of war. Where once merchants had discussed at length the finer details of their trade agreements, Imperial soldiers now patrolled, seeking to draw out their elusive foe. Where once goods were piled high, Genestealer Cultists now hid, burrowed and made their lairs. Vicious firefights broke out daily, and the smell of industry was replaced with the stench of rotting flesh.

The insidious creatures laced many corridors with traps and used every known guerrilla tactic. Patrols were ambushed and destroyed, guardsmen ripped to shreds by bestial claws and armoured columns fell into well-disguised tank traps filled with anti-armour mines. Infantry platoons reported being assaulted from all sides at once, many of them caught in deadly autogun crossfires even as purple-skinned monsters rushed to tear them limb from limb. Others came under assault for scant minutes before their attackers broke off completely and disappeared, leaving no trace. Officer after officer was assassinated, their bodies found bearing hideous blade wounds or pistol shots to the head.

Mines and other explosive devices became as prolific as the bloodsucking flies in the Leont Marshlands, and thousands upon thousands of soldiers lost limbs to them. Areas swept clear of explosives were often found riddled with them again only days later, and without the oratory and zealotry of military priests and Commissars, many of Haephos' senior officers expected their soldiers' morale to collapse beyond recovery.

A REDISCOVERY OF FAITH

The T'au first came to Haephos at the height of the fighting against the Genestealer Cult uprisings. Making their diplomatic overtures to Governor Hatiar directly, they explained that they were of the Water caste, one of five castes that made up their race.

They identified Haephos' new threat as the Genestealer Cults, explaining in detail how the T'au had engaged them on other worlds, and how they wished to form a partnership with Imperial governors to defeat this most terrible threat. At this time Hatiar was desperate; everything she had ever known appeared to be crashing down around her, and her armies were nearly bled dry by myriad foes. The stars of the night skies had changed beyond all recognition. The Imperium was out of reach.

The xenos' proposal was a tempting one. They spoke persuasively, offering the victory, peace and prosperity Hatiar desired so much. She questioned what the Imperium had ever done for her, what it was doing for her now. She was prepared to acquiesce to their offer when tidings were brought to her from an Imperial priest who had miraculously survived a terrific battle. The priest spoke of a xenos foe that fought with advanced weaponry whilst clad in enormous warsuits. They had killed Imperial soldiery and Genestealer Cultists with equal impunity.

Upon hearing this, Hatiar spurned the T'au's offer of allegiance, stating emphatically that her loyalty to the Emperor was second to nothing, and that she was a woman without price. She decried the duplicity of aliens and vowed that all would be wiped from the face of Haephos. Hatiar saw the priest's survival and message as a sign from the Emperor himself. Her faith was restored, and she took to directing the campaign for Haephos with renewed vigour.

The governor's forces had advantages of their own, however. With the wealth of the planet behind them, they were able to bring formidable numbers and firepower to bear. Hatiar's generals sought to capitalise on this and draw the enemy into open battle, presenting them with weak forces acting as lures. When they attacked infantry companies placed deliberately as bait, whole gene-cycles were wiped out by squadrons of roaring Hellhounds and deadly Valkyrie Gunships.

The Haephosians mobilised forces large enough to sweep whole swathes of Eletyrio in gigantic pincer movements. Infantry regiments and implacable armoured companies closed on certain areas of the spaceport like a vice, leaving their enemies no escape. Though these battles resulted in enormous losses for Hatiar's forces as the cultists fought for their survival like frenzied, caged animals, the strategy's overall effectiveness was hard to deny. Once it had been fully implemented, it would only be a matter of time before Eletyrio fell.

The fighting remained arduous nonetheless. Blade-limbed xenos cultists inflicted appalling damage, tearing apart Imperial infantry with frightening ease before they were put down. Hulking brutes wielding immense picks, and hammers shrugged off all but the heaviest weapons fire as they crushed their enemies to pulp. An entire Thaxarillian Guard regiment even fell to the xenos taint, turning on their allies in a terrible surprise attack. It took months of gruelling fighting to finally destroy them, in which time other units also had to be purged; the same corruption had somehow spread from the cultists to thousands of Imperial troops. Nevertheless, these were all but minor setbacks. The cultists had nowhere left to run.

Eletyrio was eventually judged secure, though sporadic fighting continued for months after the official declaration of victory. The port itself was now little more than a blasted ruin, many of the ships it had docked reduced to slag or barely valuable for scrap. Even with no other port under attack, it was doubtful that Haephos would be able to meet its tithe requirements for years. But Hatiar was optimistic. If they had won here, they could win elsewhere. They had been out of contact with the wider Imperium for years and the governor believed that, if this state of affairs continued, she would be able to rebuild and produce enough resources to meet any requirements once contact was re-established. Just as Hatiar's first smile for many months appeared on her face, she received word. A xenos fleet approached. It was the T'au.

THE VOROTHEION UPRISING

In the bowels of Vorotheion's hive cities, Genestealer Cultists of the Pauper Princes stirred. They faced not one challenger for their world, but two. Alien interlopers beguiled the Human elite, hoping to seize the planet. This could not be allowed; Vorotheion belonged to the Star Children.

The Pauper Princes were not ready to rise, but they had no choice. These were dangerous, confusing times. The powers of the Dark Gods were palpable. In opposition to them were Vorotheion's ruling elite – the Oppressors – whose deluded holy men preached louder and punished harder. Then the arrival of the T'au changed everything. Their presence threatened to shift the balance of power and destroy the Oppressor hierarchies that generations of Pauper Princes had

worked so devotedly to infiltrate. The T'au had to be stopped, and to do that Vorotheion had to be seized. All true believers knew that the Star Children would reward the Pauper Princes for their efforts, and that any hardship was worth that prize.

The tendrils of the Pauper Princes' gene-sects reached throughout Vorotheion, from hive sumps to spire tops. Yet theirs was not the only influence undermining loyalty

to the Imperial Oppressors. A new cult had emerged and was rapidly spreading, dedicated to what it called the 'Greater Good'. They too spoke of unity, of deliverance that would come from the stars. This cult had also recruited members in echelons of power. To many of the Pauper Princes' Primuses, they represented a considerable threat. Vorotheion's internal politics became embroiled in tense struggles as agents for both the Greater Good and the Star Children vied for supremacy in debates about whether or not Vorotheion should welcome the T'au.

Using their already tight claw-hold, the Pauper Princes won the fraught diplomatic battle. Miraculously, the Star Children had blessed them with more Maguses than ever before, as if they knew that their worshippers would need such help. These individuals had inveigled themselves into the upper strata of Vorotheion's elite, infiltrating councils and official meetings. Now, they used their psychic powers and domineering oratory to persuade their colleagues that an alliance with the T'au Empire was not in the planet's best interests. In the aftermath of the Great Rift's emergence the Maguses' powers had become even stronger, and they exploited these boons from the Star Children to the full. They took over the minds of many officials, casting vital votes or making rousing speeches. Where necessary, the Maguses sent the Sanctuses to those who could not be convinced.

Meanwhile, from the toxic sumps to the filthy sewers, from hot manufactoria to claustrophobic hab-blocks, the Pauper Princes prepared for war. Biophaguses implanted more and more of the populace with Genestealer germ-seed, knowing that Aberrants would be needed in their thousands in the wars to come. Tales of great masked heroes and liberators with legendary marksmanship spread throughout the underhives, stirring the oppressed masses against their overlords. Sanctuses did their bloody assassination work day after day – priests of the Imperial Creed were discovered by their acolytes with their throats slashed, Astra Militarum officers dropped dead mid-briefing after being struck by silent and toxic needler rounds and many shift leaders and bureaucrats simply vanished. Everywhere the Pauper Princes' agents worked they saw traces of the interlopers, from cheaply printed tracts on an empire of unity to hyper-technological devices hidden in jewellery.

As the Pauper Princes learned more of this so-called 'Greater Good', they could not fail to notice the similarities it bore with their own creed. The differences revealed its falseness, however, and the Pauper Princes showed many of those misled by its teachings the true way. By convincing their rivals that the multi-limbed 'Tow-vaah' they followed in fact represented the Star Children, the Pauper Princes lured many to their own cause. Clamavuses read scripture and promised brotherhood, telling tales of prophecy fulfilled and legendary uprisings. Some not persuaded by the Clamavuses' impassioned preaching were instead brought into the fold by the clarity of the Genestealer's Kiss. The T'au themselves were nowhere to be seen, unaware of how some Humans had interpreted the T'au'va, and unwilling to endorse those interpretations they did know of.

When the T'au's offer of friendship was rejected, the aliens began military action. Coordinating extensively with followers of the Greater Good on Vorotheion,

they struck primarily at the planet's principal hive, Zemirus. Many of the lead attacking cadres expected to be welcomed by their allies on the ground, enabling a rapid insertion. They were wrong. Defensive gun battery crews, though loyal, had in fact turned to the Star Children. Their deadly salvoes shot numerous T'au gunships and transports out of the sky, sending burning wreckage crashing into Vorotheion's densely clustered hab-blocks. Many T'au that successfully deployed were ambushed as they disembarked from their transports, Fire Warriors and Crisis suits cut apart as waves of hybrids and Aberrants descended upon them in a predatory frenzy. Not all of the T'au were so easily overcome, however. Those who were part of the Fourth Sphere Expansion had little care for any expected Human welcome, and made assault landings regardless. Conducting detailed drills, these T'au cadres cut down hundreds of rushing cultists with precision pulse-fire to secure a beachhead. Fifth Sphere Cadres with particularly aggressive commanders also made successful landfall, though all were immensely hard-pressed. The veil of secrecy that the Pauper Princes had fought hard to maintain until this point was lifted; they now made themselves known to T'au and Oppressor alike, and their full uprising was impossible to hold back.

All over Zemirus, the true colours of dozens of Vorotheion defence regiments were revealed. Thousands of troops carved a bloody path through barracks and fortifications, cleansing them of any personnel untouched by the Star Children's beneficence. Brutal hand-to-hand combat broke out between the belligerents – soldiers who only hours before had been allies stabbing bayonets into each other's guts, or throttling their former comrades on the blood-wet iron floors. The murderous underhive, always a place of

'Offspring of the Star Children, I bid you rise.

Usurpers come to wrest our world from our oppressors' hands. We will stop them.

Vorotheion is our entitlement. Our legacy. It is not theirs to take.

Their cretinous, fraudulent and feeble creed already crawls amongst the weak of this place. Those who are easily confused and misled, we will enlighten.

We know the Star Children's will. Prepare for their arrival. Prepare for ascension. How would our divine lieges have us do this? Remember: blessed are the oppressed. Beatified are the persecuted. Raised are the war-makers.'

- Mallik Valka, Clamavus

wanton violence, became a scene of total war. Icons raised high, cultists surged through hive slums and manufactoria under the guidance of their Primuses and Nexoses, the tactical genius of their leadership far in excess of that of the gangers and enforcers standing against them.

On every level of Hive Zemirus, conflict raged. Vorotheion Fusiliers clashed with the Brothers of the Bloodied Helix and the Disciples of the Coil in the Galleries of Paikon, the vast exhibitions of priceless art and artefacts playing host to acts of terrible bloodshed as claw-limbed beasts wielded powerful mining tools as weapons. Such was the ubiquity of the cultists that the Fusiliers were forced to use flamers to burn them out, putting to the torch relics thousands of years

<<Vox Recording
Intercepted —
Prioritas Nihil:
Rumor Malignas>>

Children of the Eighth Brood Cycle. Brothers and Sisters in service of the Great Father. Our beloved sire grants you a task, one of vital import in our quest to seize our birthright and overthrow those who would see us crushed beneath their steel-shod heels.

Long have the jackboots of the 11th Vorotheion Life Guards oppressed us. Long have they murdered our families and exploited our labour. This will end. You and many others will be their destruction. You will taste their fears, slice their cruel smiles from their bitter faces and bleed them dry. You will leave none alive.

The sire has selected you himself. You are his chosen ones. The ones called to this undertaking. The great Star Children shall reward you for your efforts. To those who carry out their sacred will, their generosity knows no bounds.

In the name of the Holy Coilfather. Strike.

++END RECORDING++

old in their efforts. The air was choked with the fumes of burning promethium and cultist corpses, but the Brothers and Disciples were tenacious. Again and again they attacked, slaughtering thousands until the hollowed-out shells of the galleries were finally seized in the name of the Star Children.

The Great Garden of Siphax – a huge, verdant landscape somehow preserved on the polluted world by unknowable ancient technology – was turned into a hellish quagmire as Goliath Rockgrinders and other vehicles of the Ironwyrm Earth-eaters clashed with the Siphaxian Honoured's armoured companies. Sentinels were shredded by the Goliaths' drilldozer blades before being crushed beneath the mining vehicles' heavy tyres. But the Genestealer Cultists were not without significant losses of their own. Countless hybrids were eradicated as their vehicles were turned to little more than metallic mulch by the melta cannons of fast-moving Devil Dogs. The battlefield itself was an enemy to both sides, the fighting having shattered macro-pipes siphoning industrial run-off away from the Great Garden. Hundreds of vehicles fell victim to the thick mud churned up as a result, their crews drowning as they were sucked into its stinking depths.

T'au forces continued to strike amongst the chaotic warfare that had consumed Zemirus' every level. Though they had failed to gain a true foothold, they were a thorn in the Pauper Princes' side. Their forces were adaptable, motivated and fast-moving, and their weapons were powerful. Streams of repeating pulse weapon fire consumed swathes of Neophyte Hybrids, while lethal fusion technology simply erased

Aberrants from existence. In this fight the T'au were prepared to stand shoulder to shoulder with the Imperial garrison, though few expected the alliance to survive the defeat of the Pauper Princes.

All of these battles were secondary, however. One target above all stood out to the Pauper Princes' Patriarchs: they had to seize Zemirus' primary generatorium. Whilst this remained in the Oppressors' hands, power could be denied to many of the hive's regions, including those fully in the Pauper Princes' claws. The Primuses could not countenance such a vulnerability which, if exploited, could result in the murder of millions of their kin and the failure of their uprising. Hundreds of thousands of cultists attacked, led by a Patriarch and a number of Maguses.

The generatorium was a huge complex of raging furnaces, thrumming reactors and rapidly-spinning turbines. The Oppressors were fully aware of its vital importance, and the regiments defending it were amongst the finest on the planet. Its workers, who lived in densely packed hab-blocks on the generatorium site itself, were themselves hardened people from whom the Oppressors recruited a tough and uncompromising militia.

The Pauper Princes' first steps were to isolate the generatorium. Distraction attacks were launched all over Zemirus to further divide the enemy. These diversionary actions meant that, when the attack came, it was all but impossible for Imperial relief forces to make it through. The Pauper Princes assaulted from every direction, Clamavuses spurring on the cultists to attack with unbridled ferocity. Squadrons of captured Leman Russ battle tanks assailed gates and walls head-on, battle cannons roaring. Such actions distracted the defenders while Purestrain Genestealers scuttled out from sewer drains and disused service tunnels to cut down the foe in droves, using their immense dexterity to scale defences and buildings. No Human was out of their predatory reach.

It was of paramount importance to the Primuses that the generatorium was captured in as intact a form as possible. Not only would this safeguard their own holdings, but it would enable them to control power levels in those areas of the hive that remained under Imperial control.

The Nexoses, formidable tacticians and fiercely intelligent feared that the Imperials might utilise the generatorium's self-destruct function to deny the Pauper Princes their prize. Ahead of the uprising, some of the generatorium's Human workers had been inducted into the cult and had managed to infiltrate the site's hierarchy. At

the desired moment, these hidden agents struck down their former colleagues with concealed blades, or opened crucial passageways to allow Sanctuses and the Kelermorph into secure locations.

Wherever the Maguses walked, Imperial troops attacked each other, their minds seized and forced to carry out terrible acts of treachery. Many others were left dumbfounded, sent into trance-like states that left them as easy prey for cultist troops, who ripped them apart with wicked claws and talons or gunned them down in cold blood. With their newfound power the Maguses imbued their followers with incredible strength. Cultists overpowered defenders at every turn, with even Neophytes capable of wrenching arms from sockets and punching straight through flak armour.

Zemirus' generatorium fell. Every one of the Pauper Princes' many arms had played a key role in its

downfall, demonstrating perfectly the power of the Star Children and the blessings they bestowed upon their offspring. With this victory achieved, the Pauper Princes rapidly increased the ferociousness of their war to seize Zemirus, and the last defenders fell scant months later.

Whilst this in itself was a remarkable feat, many hives still stood across Vorotheion – some in the hands of the T'au Empire, others still in Imperial control after throwing down the uprisings they faced. A number of these fell in a matter of days, such was the Pauper Princes' prevalence. Others fought on, selling their lives dearly.

Genestealer Cult agents of all kinds had been galvanised by the challenge ahead, carrying out their gods-given tasks with deep fervour. Nonetheless, the Pauper Princes had much work left to do to bring about the arrival of the Star Children.

Echoes of Awakening

The disastrous effects of the Great Rift, the psychic wound that spans the breadth of the galaxy, are still being counted. Disparate events hundreds of light years apart have traits in common that those Imperial agents piecing together scraps of vox-bursts, astropathic signals and other data are only now beginning to understand.

+++

```
Maj. Z.B. Epra
Unides-eta Evacuation MISSID
52:15PW — GZ North

Epsilon Company in sector omega-two-five
reports successful rout of Aeldari light
reconnaissance elements. Guardsman Ortug
lauded for 'miraculous' identification of
foe waiting in ambush position.

In accordance with new directive 616Δ,
Guardsman Ortug has been reported to
Battalion Commissariat for 'behaviour
believed highly suspicious' in light of
recent anomalous and heretical events.

Chi Company's 4th Platoon is destroyed,
following discovery of ancient Aeldari
relic armour. Armour apparently recovered
by enemy before incineration could take
place. The scant Human remains suggest
attackers of the 'Warp Spider' warrior
caste. Chi Company commander summarily
executed for lack of foresight and
failure to place adequate guard.
```

+++

```
Prioritas Ultima \\001A
Category: Sacris Theftus
```

Grand Master Voldus, the ritual is ceased. The Cyclops' plans are undone. But a handful of us escaped. The Supreme Grand Master himself aided us. Without him, we would know naught but failure and death.

I bear grave tidings. The body of every lost brother is unrecovered. Their gene-seed is entirely lost to us. To say none has fallen into the Crimson King's clutches would be foolhardy at best. I can only beg for forgiveness for my failure. I dare not think what that monster would do with our brothers' legacy. A reckoning is needed.

+++

The Four-armed Emperor is the Greater Good! Behold the similarities. Hear what they both wish for their people. Peace, unity, a new age, a time of joy and prosperity free from oppression, where all have purpose and place!

+++

[Vox Intercept: Cruor, Sub-sector Straziar]

'KILL! MAIM! BURN! KILL! MAIM! BURN! KILL! MAIM! BURN! KILL! MAIM! BURN! KILL! MAIM! BURN! KILL! MAIM! BURN! KILL! MAIM! BURN! KILL! MAIM! BURN! KILL! MAIM! BURN! KILL! MAIM! BURN! KILL! MAIM! BURN! KILL! MAIM! BURN! KILL! MAIM! BURN! KILL! MAIM! BURN! KILL! MAIM! BURN! KILL! MAIM! BURN!'

Addendum: Vox transmission has been continuous for approximately four solar months and counting. QR and SM dispatched separately to investigate. All contact lost with both. PN and UF-3 to investigate.

+++

The mechanical gods stride! With each mighty step they tread on those who once trod on us! Join them in their glorious endeavour; may vengeance be ours and may our oppressors be toppled!

+++

Intelligentus Xenos Incursio: Agrax Approximatus

Archmagos Cawl, blackstone extraction missions in the vicinity of the Agrax System have failed to meet the previous forty-three scheduled report updates. A single broken message has come through, its quality deeply unsatisfactory. Zyto-Neumann-2918, a Skitarius of low rank, claims that the dig site was attacked not only by Necron forces – accounted for in blackstone recovery expeditions as my lord knows – but also by xenos classed as Drukhari. These interloping xenos, the Skitarius claims, slew a great many of our assets and escaped with considerable volumes of blackstone. Why they did this is subject to conjecture at this time.

Events in the Prosperan Rift

Our mission was successful, Supreme Grand Master Azrael. Magnus' ritual was halted before it could conclude, but the Prosperan Rift is engulfed in war. Magnus' influence runs deep there.

Crucially, the Grey Knights did not pry into our affairs, nor were we given any reason to believe they know more than they should. Our future in this respect remains secure.

The 5th Company is badly mauled, however. Many dead were left behind, and with great shame I report that some of our brothers could not be evacuated. Much gene-seed has been lost. I submit myself to your judgement.

+++

```
Vox Echo:
Unknown Flesh Tearers Vessel
Location: Red Scar Proximatus


Our... new brothers. The returned
Primarch's... gift to us. They are as
vulnerable as any of us to the Angel's
legacy. To think that some heralded these
as some 'great hope'. It is sickening. It
is shameful. Let us hope the atonement
they earn in death is worth more than
their ignominy in life.
```

+++

Intercepted comms burst 73∂∏/29ΣΔ — Escalate. Prioritas Primus.

We are under attack. Heretic Astartes-class foe. Uniforms and heraldry identified on approximately 78.6% of recorded enemies indicate they are of the Iron Warriors. Scores of anomalous reports have been filed of myriad 'engine-beasts' (full classifications of eleven plus varieties yet to be made – all unknown to the Adeptus Mechanicus). Engine-beasts claimed to be in possession of empyric-grade weapons and munitions. Numerous macroclades destroyed, seven forge-fanes under direct assault, twenty-three under imminent threat. All macroclades to be mustered. Aid is requested. Repeat, aid is requested.

+++

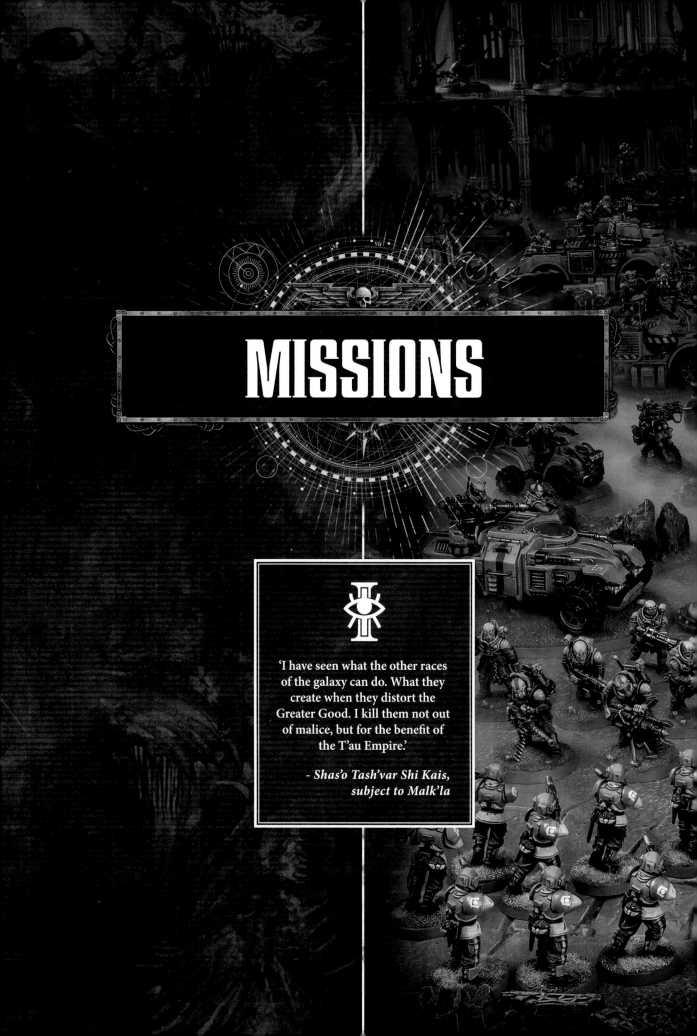

MISSIONS

'I have seen what the other races of the galaxy can do. What they create when they distort the Greater Good. I kill them not out of malice, but for the benefit of the T'au Empire.'

- Shas'o Tash'var Shi Kais,
subject to Malk'la

WARS OF THE FIFTH SPHERE

The rules presented in this section allow you to play games set in locations inspired by those found in the narrative of this book, as well as play through one of the most dramatic and climactic moments during the Psychic Awakening, when the T'au Empire began its assault upon the Imperial world of Astorgius.

INTRODUCTION

This section starts by providing a new Theatre of War, shown opposite, that is designed to represent any one of the numerous caverns found beneath the surface of Haephos. Hollowed out by centuries of mining operations, fighting within these closed-in environs is fraught with great danger, but sometimes the most critical victories are won in the darkest of places.

These rules can, however, be used to represent any location where there is a large enough break in a tunnel network, be it naturally occurring or artificially

formed, to allow for two armies to bring their forces to bear against one another.

On pages 26-27, a new historical battle is presented for use in narrative play. The Taking of Iglesor Magna lets players fight through the final moments of Commander Shadowsun's all out assault on that hugely symbolic city, as the Imperials try desperately to hold the T'au forces back. The mission describes how to lay out the battlefield in order to best reflect this specific battlefront, and provides new rules and Stratagems for use in this scenario.

'The Nem'yar Atoll is ours for the taking. It is by a strange twist of science that we now dwell here, and it is a testament to our adaptability and surety of purpose that we thrive in doing so. Some say that this has been among our race's greatest tests – if they are right, I do not hesitate to say that the T'au'va has passed even beyond our highest expectations.'

- Aun'el T'au Shoh Ko'vash

THEATRES OF WAR

In this section you will find an exciting new Theatre of War to use in your games of Warhammer 40,000. Theatres of War offer new tactical challenges to enrich your games, and introduce new rules to represent many varied battle environments. Some modify the core rules, for example by altering the range of weapons. Some provide new rules for phenomena like dust storms, volcanic eruptions and earthquakes. Some grant additional abilities and Stratagems to certain units.

These rules are designed to reflect the unstable and claustrophobic nature of underground warfare on Haephos, but they are entirely optional and, so long as you and your opponent agree, they can be used in any Warhammer 40,000 game, set anywhere.

Agree which, if any, Theatre of War rules will be used when you are setting up the battlefield, before deployment.

THEATRE OF WAR: CAVERN WARFARE

Many Imperial worlds of the Nem'yar Atoll and the Chalnath Expanse have ancient histories of mining and industry, leaving them riddled with labyrinthine tunnels and cavernous voids that have witnessed desperate underground battles.

Low Ceiling: Neither player's army can contain any models with the Flyer Battlefield Role.

Cave-in: At the start of each player's turn, the player whose turn is taking place must select one unit from their army and roll one D6; on a 5+ that unit suffers D3 mortal wounds and this process ends. On a 1-4 that player repeats this process, selecting a unit from their army that has not yet been rolled for. If all units in that player's army have been rolled for, this process ends.

No Place to Hide: When resolving an attack made against a unit that contains any models with a Wounds characteristic of 10 or higher, add 1 to the hit roll.

Close Confines: When resolving an attack made with a ranged weapon that has a random Damage characteristic, add 1 to the damage roll.

ECHOES OF WAR
THE TAKING OF IGLESOR MAGNA

Iglesor Magna was the most magnificent cathedra-city of the cardinal world Astorgius, whose architectural beauty, priceless treasures and formidable military capabilities garnered awe throughout the sector. To demonstrate the power of the T'au'va, Shadowsun deemed that the city should fall.

THE ARMIES

Each player must first muster an army from their collection. The Defender commands the regiments of the Astra Militarum, representing the guerilla defenders of Iglesor Magna; their army cannot include more than one of each datasheet with the **Vehicle** keyword, and cannot include any models with the Lord of War Battlefield Role.

The Attacker commands a force of the T'au Empire, led by Commander Shadowsun. If the players' armies are Battle-forged, they will also be able to use the appropriate Stratagems included with this mission (see opposite).

THE BATTLEFIELD

The Defender creates the battlefield. The battlefield should feature a mix of buildings and roads to represent the basilica district. An objective marker should be placed, as shown on the map here, to mark the location of the Astra Militarum's last stand.

DEPLOYMENT

After terrain has been set up, the Attacker sets up their units wholly within their deployment zone. The Defender then sets up their units wholly within their deployment zone. Both players can set up units in Reserve (pg 194, *Warhammer 40,000 Rulebook*). The combined Power Rating of the units each player sets up in Reserve cannot exceed half of their army's Power Level.

The Defender then places two secret passage markers anywhere on the battlefield outside of the Attacker's deployment zone.

FIRST TURN

The Attacker has the first turn.

SECRET PASSAGES

Units from the Defender's army that arrive from Reserve must be set up wholly within 6" of any secret passage markers, and not within 1" of any enemy units.

STAUNCH RESOLVE

When taking a Morale test for a unit from the Defender's army, subtract 2 from the result.

BATTLE LENGTH

Use the Random Battle Length rules (pg 194, *Warhammer 40,000 Rulebook*) to determine how long the battle lasts.

VICTORY CONDITIONS

At the end of the battle, whichever player controls the objective marker wins a major victory.

Attacker's Battlefield Edge

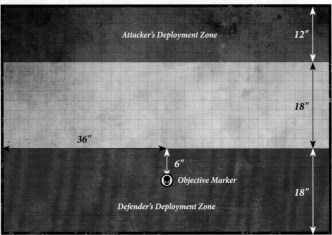

Attacker's Deployment Zone — 12"

18"

36"

6"

Objective Marker

18"

Defender's Deployment Zone

Defender's Battlefield Edge

STRATAGEMS

In this mission, the players can use Command Points (CPs) to use the following bonus Stratagems:

SWIFT ADVANCE
1CP

Attacker Stratagem

In the intense fighting for Iglesor Magna, the T'au are swift to take any advantage they can.

Use this Stratagem at the start of your Movement phase. Select up to three **T'au Empire** units from your army. Until the end of that phase, when one of those units Advances, add 6" to its Move characteristic instead of making an Advance roll.

PREPARED TRAPS
1CP

Defender Stratagem

Iglesor Magna's defenders know how to exploit every defensible point of their cathedra-city, deploying countless mines and traps to hinder the T'au advance.

Use this Stratagem in your opponent's Movement phase, after they make a move with a unit from their army that does not have the **Character** keyword. That unit suffers D6 mortal wounds. You can only use this Stratagem once per battle.

BREAKING THEIR SPIRIT
0CP

Attacker Stratagem

The T'au are determined to break their foes' morale. A quick victory will inspire fear in the other cathedra-cities and bolster the T'au fighting elsewhere.

Use this Stratagem in the Shooting or Fight phase, when an enemy **Character** unit is destroyed as a result of an attack made by a **T'au Empire** model from your army. You receive 1 Command Point.

UNEXPECTED AMBUSH
1CP

Defender Stratagem

The warriors who defend Iglesor Magna know every inch of their fortress' secret passageways, halls and corridors, and use them to launch ambush after ambush against the T'au invaders and their allies.

Use this Stratagem in your Movement phase, after an **Astra Militarum** unit from your army is set up on the battlefield. Until the end of that turn, when resolving an attack made by a model in that unit, add 1 to the hit roll.

UNDER THE COVER OF DARKNESS
1CP

Attacker Stratagem

Blacksun filters help the T'au excel in combat in pitch darkness.

Use this Stratagem at the start of the first battle round, before the first turn begins. Select one **T'au Empire** unit from your army. That unit can make a move as if it were your Movement phase. That unit must end that move more than 9" away from any enemy models. If both players have units that can do this, the player who is taking the first turn moves their units first.

RESOLUTE DEFENDERS
2CP

Defender Stratagem

No matter what the forces of the T'au Empire throw at them, the defenders of Iglesor Magna stand firm, rarely giving an inch of ground without a tough fight.

Use this Stratagem at the start of the Morale phase. Until the end of that phase, when a Morale test is taken for an **Astra Militarum** unit from your army within 12" of the objective marker, do not roll the dice; it is automatically passed.

T'AU EMPIRE

'On some level, almost all creatures know the Greater Good. It is a concept beyond race and species. It is but our task to open their eyes to what has been before them all along.'

- Por'vre Dal'yth Ukos, Water caste envoy

SERVANTS OF THE GREATER GOOD

This section contains new and updated rules for the T'au Empire, including a datasheet for Commander Shadowsun, a range of tenets for creating custom T'au Septs, Prototype Weapons Systems, Stratagems, and rules for fielding the Farsight Enclaves and their greatest living champions, the Eight.

This section is a supplement to *Codex: T'au Empire* – you will need a copy of that book to use the rules in this section.

Name Generator

Opposite you will find a useful tool to help you name your T'au warriors, further building the background and personality of your army.

Commander Shadowsun

Page 33 presents a revised datasheet for Commander Shadowsun, the most famous Fire caste commander.

Sept Tenets

Pages 34-35 present a selection of abilities that can be combined to create a T'au Sept of your own devising, or to represent a Sept from the Warhammer 40,000 background that is not represented by a Sept Tenet in *Codex: T'au Empire*.

Prototype Weapons Systems

T'au engineers are constantly adapting and improving their race's already impressive technology. Pages 36-37 present rules for equipping a unit in your army with unique prototype weapons systems.

Stratagems

If your army is Battle-forged and includes any T'AU EMPIRE Detachments, the Stratagems on pages 38-39 can be used in addition to those presented in the codex, bringing a new range of tactical options to the architects of the Greater Good.

The Eight

The Eight are a renowned group of warriors who have fought alongside Commander Farsight for years. Pages 46-49 present rules for using these mighty fighters in your battles.

Farsight Enclaves

Pages 50-53 present rules enabling you to field the forces of the breakaway Farsight Enclaves faction, including abilities, Stratagems, Relics, Warlord Traits and Tactical Objectives.

T'AU EMPIRE NAME GENERATOR

If you wish to create a name for one of your T'au warriors you can use the tables below, picking your preferred compenents or rolling a D66 to determine a name. To roll a D66, roll two D6, one after the other – the first represents tens and the second represents digits, giving you a result between 11 and 66.

CASTE

T'au names are multipart, with the prefix that names the caste they were born into considered by far to be the most important part.

Shas – Fire (soldiers and warriors)
Fio – Earth (engineers and scientists)
Kor – Air (pilots and starfarers)
Por – Water (diplomats and merchants)

RANK

The second component in a T'au name communicates the bearer's rank, presented below in ascending order of seniority.

'la – Warrior
'ui – Veteran
'vre – Hero
'el – Noble (possibly knight)
'o – Commander

SEPT

The third component in a T'au name indicates the sept in which they were born, raised and trained.

T'au
Dal'yth
T'au'n
Fal'shia
D'yanoi
Vior'la
Bork'an
Au'taal
Tash'var
N'dras
Vash'ya
Ke'lshan
T'olku
Elsy'er
Fi'rios
Mu'gulath Bay
Fe'saan
Kor'tal
Yo'vai
Sa'cea
Ksi'm'yen

T'AU INDIVIDUAL NAME GENERATOR

D66	NAME
11	Sul'an
12	Ho'sen
13	Atsumo
14	N'ea
15	Els'im
16	K'yen
21	Or'os
22	Pashera
23	Rais
24	Sel'tas
25	Be'tol
26	E'yaal
31	Murakan
32	To'jo
33	Kurami
34	U'so
35	Lorresa
36	Paluto
41	Ren'as
42	Lor'ma
43	Tash'lor
44	Watana
45	Nomura
46	Nishino
51	D'tano
52	Xo'yima
53	T'suka
54	Kais
55	Shamasa
56	Pu'jato
61	Ju'yem
62	Ga'mo
63	Kasashi
64	Lamano
65	Mi'daro
66	Uvash'a

COMMANDER SHADOWSUN

HERO OF THE THIRD SPHERE EXPANSION, SPEARHEAD OF THE GREATER GOOD, THE TRUE DISCIPLE OF COMMANDER PURETIDE

O'Shaserra, also known as Commander Shadowsun, is a dynamic leader who rose to fame in the battles of the K'resh Expansions against the Orks. All of Shadowsun's victories are marked by unrivalled efficiency, a trait not surprising from one of Commander Puretide's most promising pupils.

Over four hundred years ago, O'Shaserra was a brilliant young warrior, her matchless performances at the Fire caste academies earning her recognition as one of the most able military minds in the T'au Empire. As such, she was granted the honour of studying personally under the ailing but legendary Commander Puretide. Despite being the youngest of Puretide's protégés, O'Shaserra scored exceptionally well in every simulation,

outstripping almost all others. Upon Commander Puretide's death, it was decided that O'Shaserra and several of his other top students would be placed in stasis, to ensure his teachings were preserved for future generations. O'Shaserra would sleep in frozen animation, untouched by the passing years, to be revived only at times of crisis. Although Aun'Va had planned to awaken her at the dawn of the Third Sphere Expansion, the largest Ork invasion of the T'au Empire

accelerated the Ethereal Supreme's careful calculations. Appearing at this time of great need, O'Shaserra proved herself a patient hunter, meticulous in her planning, yet swift in action.

O'Shaserra is a superlative warrior and a masterful tactician. She leaps around the battlefield in her XV22 battlesuit, using its advanced targeting systems and sophisticated cloaking technology to identify her prey and stalk them unseen. With her wide array of deadly weapons she is the bane of almost any foe – her fusion blasters make a mockery of heavy armour, her missile pod cracks open light vehicles and her flechette launcher shreds any who get too close with a hail of razor-sharp shot.

When the T'au Empire re-established contact with the lost Fourth Sphere Expansion, Commander Shadowsun was again revived from stasis to lead the mission to reunite with them. Known as the Fifth Sphere Expansion, the armada assembled on her order ventured into the unknown of the Startide Nexus to find their lost kin. Though the reunion was far from the celebratory one all had hoped for, Shadowsun nevertheless took command of the T'au of the Nem'yar Atoll, advancing the cause of the T'au'va far from the empire proper. Since defending the Startide Nexus from an attack by the Death Guard, Shadowsun's forces have fortified more distant regions of space and established numerous colonies and Septs. A new era of expansion has begun for the T'au, and Shadowsun will be at its forefront.

COMMANDER SHADOWSUN

NAME	M	WS	BS	S	T	W	A	Ld	Sv
Commander Shadowsun	8"	3+	2+	4	4	5	4	9	3+
MV37 Advanced Guardian Drone	8"	5+	5+	3	4	1	1	6	4+
MV62 Command-link Drone	8"	5+	5+	3	4	1	1	6	4+

Commander Shadowsun is a single model equipped with: flechette launcher; 2 high-energy fusion blasters; light missile pod; pulse pistol. This model is accompanied by 1 MV37 Advanced Guardian Drone and 1 MV62 Command-link Drone. You can only include one of this model in your army.

WEAPON	RANGE	TYPE	S	AP	D	ABILITIES
Dispersed fusion blaster	18"	Assault 2	7	-4	D3	When resolving an attack made with this weapon against a unit that is within half range, roll one additional D3 when inflicting damage with it and discard one of the dice.
Flechette launcher	18"	Pistol 5	3	0	1	-
High-energy fusion blaster	24"	Assault 1	8	-4	D6	When resolving an attack made with this weapon against a unit that is within half range, roll one additional D6 when inflicting damage with it and discard one of the dice.
Light missile pod	24"	Assault 2	7	-1	D3	-
Pulse pistol	12"	Pistol 1	5	0	1	-

WARGEAR OPTIONS	• For each high-energy fusion blaster this model is equipped with, it can instead be equipped with 1 dispersed fusion blaster.

ABILITIES (SHADOWSUN)	For the Greater Good, Master of War (see *Codex: T'au Empire*) **Defender of the Greater Good:** When this model would lose any wounds as a result of an attack whilst this model is within 3" of a friendly **XV25 Stealth Battlesuits** unit, that unit can attempt to intercept that attack. Roll one D6; on a 2+ this model does not lose those wounds and that unit suffers 1 mortal wound for each of those wounds. Only one attempt can be made to intercept each attack. **Supreme Commander:** This model can be included in a **T'au Empire** Detachment without preventing other units in that Detachment from gaining a Sept Tenet. Note, however, that this model does not benefit from any Sept Tenet unless the Sept Tenet selected for that Detachment is Coordinated Fire Arcs. **Infiltrator:** When you set up this model and its accompanying **Drones** during deployment, they can be set up anywhere on the battlefield that is more than 12" away from the enemy deployment zone and any enemy models.	**Genius of Kauyon:** Once per battle, this model can declare Kauyon even if Kauyon or Mont'ka has already been declared. Mont'ka and Kauyon cannot both be declared in the same turn. **Command-link Drone:** At the start of your Shooting phase, if a friendly **Command-link Drone** model is within 3" of this model, select one friendly **T'au Empire** unit within 12" of that model. Until the end of that phase, when resolving an attack made by a model in that **T'au Empire** unit, you can re-roll a hit roll of 1. **Drone Support:** When this model is set up on the battlefield, its accompanying **Drone** models are set up in unit coherency with it. From that point onwards, the **Drone** models are treated as a separate unit. **Camouflage Fields:** When resolving an attack made with a ranged weapon against this model or any accompanying **Drones**, subtract 1 from the hit roll. **XV22 Stalker Battlesuit:** This model has a 5+ invulnerable save.

ABILITIES (COMMAND-LINK DRONE)	For the Greater Good (see *Codex: T'au Empire*) **Saviour Protocols:** When resolving an attack made against a \<Sept\> **Infantry** or \<Sept\> **Battlesuit** unit whilst that unit is within 3" of a friendly \<Sept\> **Drones** unit, if the wound roll is successful, you can roll one D6; on a 2+ that **Drones** unit suffers 1 mortal wound and the attack sequence ends.		

ABILITIES (ADVANCED GUARDIAN DRONE)	For the Greater Good (see *Codex: T'au Empire*) **Advanced Guardian Field:** This model has a 4+ invulnerable save. When a friendly **T'au Empire** model would lose a wound whilst within 3" of this model, roll one D6; on a 6 that wound is not lost.	**Saviour Protocols:** When resolving an attack made against a \<Sept\> **Infantry** or \<Sept\> **Battlesuit** unit whilst that unit is within 3" of a friendly \<Sept\> **Drones** unit, if the wound roll is successful, you can roll one D6; on a 2+ that **Drones** unit suffers 1 mortal wound and the attack sequence ends.

FACTION KEYWORDS	**T'au Empire, T'au Sept**

KEYWORDS (SHADOWSUN)	**Infantry, Battlesuit, Character, Commander, XV22 Stalker, Jet Pack, Fly, Shadowsun**

KEYWORDS (COMMAND-LINK DRONE)	**Drone, Fly, Command-link Drone**

KEYWORDS (ADVANCED GUARDIAN DRONE)	**Drone, Fly, Advanced Guardian Drone**

SEPT TENETS

As the T'au Empire has inexorably expanded across the stars, more and more planets have been colonised and become sept worlds. The septs have all developed their own unique ways of war, shaped by technological advancement, rigorous combat testing and the many battles they have fought.

Codex: T'au Empire describes how the <Sept> keyword can be substituted with the name of your chosen sept, as well as describing the abilities that units in T'AU EMPIRE Detachments gain. One of these abilities is Sept Tenets. If your chosen sept does not have an associated Sept Tenet in *Codex: T'au Empire*, you can create its Sept Tenet by selecting two rules from the following list:

Turbo-jets

The T'au of some septs relish the immense manoeuvrability of their battlesuits more than others, and equip them with advanced jets.

Add 1 to Advance rolls made for JET PACK units with this tenet. Add 2" to the Move characteristic of JET PACK models with this tenet.

Dedication to the Cause

The Greater Good is a cause greater than any T'au or even any caste. It is the perfect ideal, one worth not only fighting for but laying down one's life for.

Add 1 to the Leadership characteristic of models with this tenet.

Soldiers in Arms

The academies of the Fire caste emphasise coordination in battle. The Fire Warriors of some septs take this further than others, working together in perfect synergy.

Increase the range of the For the Greater Good ability to 9" for units with this tenet.

Stabilisation Systems

The threats that stand against the T'au Empire are myriad. To defeat them requires speed and firepower in equal measure.

When resolving an attack made with a ranged weapon by a BATTLESUIT model with this tenet, that model does not suffer the penalty for moving and firing Heavy weapons.

Hardened Warheads

Any enemy of the T'au Empire soon learns to fear its incredible firepower. Some septs take this to the extreme, utilising even more formidable missile systems.

When resolving an attack made with a high-yield missile pod, missile pod, seeker missile, or smart missile

system by a model with this tenet, improve the Armour Penetration characteristic of that weapon by 1 for that attack (e.g. AP 0 becomes AP -1).

Sophisticated Command Net

Efficiency is always strived for by the T'au. To make every shot count, the vehicle crews of this sept use an advanced communications net to know where markerlights will be placed ahead of time.

When resolving an attack made by a **Vehicle** model with this tenet against a unit that has one or more markerlight counters, re-roll a wound roll of 1.

Hybridised Weaponry

The T'au of this sept are experts in close-quarters fighting, and have customised their weapons with enhanced power packs, grenade launchers and other equipment to make them even more effective.

Add 4" to the Range characteristic of Assault and Grenade weapons models with this tenet are equipped with. This does not apply to Prototype Weapons Systems.

Gifted Pilots

Mastery of battle tanks and the largest battlesuits is seen as the mark of a true warrior by the T'au of this sept.

If, in your Movement phase, a **Vehicle** or **Monster** model with this tenet does not move or moves a distance less than half its Move characteristic, until the end of the turn, when resolving an attack made with a ranged weapon by that model, re-roll a wound roll of 1.

Advanced Power Cells

Some septs have relatively small populations, and rely more heavily on drones to support them in battle. Many upgrade their faithful helpers to this end.

Tactical Drones models with this tenet have a Move characteristic of 10".

Manoeuvring Thrusters

The battlesuit pilots of some septs use specialised thrusters to dart in and out of combat, engaging the enemy at extreme close range before withdrawing at speed.

A **Battlesuit** unit with this tenet can Advance when it Falls Back.

Up-gunned

On battlefield after battlefield, the burst cannon has proven its worth against uncounted foes. Able to slaughter light infantry with ease, many T'au upgrade the weapon to be capable of punching through armoured targets.

Burst cannons models with this tenet are equipped with have an Armour Penetration characteristic of -1.

PROTOTYPE WEAPONS SYSTEMS

If a T'au Empire **Character** is your Warlord, rather than giving one of your T'au Empire **Character** models a Signature System from *Codex: T'au Empire*, you can instead select a Prototype Weapons System for one T'au Empire unit from your army. To do so, before the battle begins select one T'au Empire unit from your army, and select a Prototype Weapons System from the list below. That Prototype Weapons System applies to the selected unit until the end of the battle. Named characters cannot be given any of the following Prototype Weapons Systems.

Note that some Prototype Weapons Systems are weapons that replace one or more existing weapons. Where this is the case, you must, if you are using points values, still pay the cost of the weapon that is being replaced. Write down any Prototype Weapons Systems your units have on your army roster.

REACTIVE COUNTERMEASURES

The battlesuit pilot unleashes a storm of fragmentation to impede incoming enemy fire.

Battlesuit model with airbursting fragmentation projector only. Ranged weapons with an Armour Penetration characteristic of -1 or -2 are treated as having an Armour Penetration characteristic of 0 when resolving attacks against a model with this Weapon System.

FUSION OBLITERATOR

Developed in response to the Imperium's immense armoured regiments, the fusion obliterator's advanced power cells give it a superior range, power and rate of fire.

XV95 Ghostkeel Battlesuit model only. This Weapon System replaces a fusion collider and has the following profile:

WEAPON	RANGE	TYPE	S	AP	D
Fusion obliterator	24"	Heavy 3	9	-4	D6
Abilities: When resolving an attack made with this weapon against a unit that is within half range, roll one additional D6 when inflicting damage with it and discard one of the dice.					

ADVANCED EM SCRAMBLER

The alien race of the Nin'aenh possessed the uncanny ability to scramble electrical systems with a single touch. Defeated after a brutal war, the Earth caste have worked tirelessly to integrate their abilities with technology.

XV95 Ghostkeel Battlesuit model only. Enemy units that are set up on the battlefield as reinforcements cannot be set up within 12" of this model.

HIGH-CAPACITANCE RAILGUN

This hyper-advanced railgun's super-conductive electrodes allow for remarkable recharge rates, doubling the weapon's rate of fire.

TX7 Hammerhead Gunship model equipped with a railgun only. This Weapon System replaces a railgun and has the following profile:

WEAPON	RANGE	TYPE	S	AP	D
High-capacitance railgun					
When you choose this weapon to shoot with, select one of the profiles below.					
- Solid shot	60"	Heavy 2	10	-4	D6
- Submunitions	60"	Heavy 4D3	6	-1	1
Abilities: When resolving an attack made with the solid shot profile, a wound roll of 6+ inflicts D3 mortal wounds on the target in addition to any other damage.					

GATLING BURST CANNON

This burst cannon is augmented with additional power accelerators and recoil absorption modules, enabling it to unleash more firepower with every deadly salvo.

Commander, XV8 Crisis Battlesuits, XV8 Crisis Bodyguards or **XV95 Ghostkeel Battlesuit** unit only. This Weapon System replaces each burst cannon that models in this unit are equipped with and has the following profile:

WEAPON	RANGE	TYPE	S	AP	D
Gatling burst cannon	18"	Assault 4	5	0	1
Abilities: When resolving an attack made with this weapon, an unmodified hit roll of 6 scores 1 additional hit.					

NETWORKED MARKERLIGHTS

These markerlights are integrated with sophisticated tracking AI, allowing for rapid targeting.

PATHFINDER TEAM unit only. This Weapon System replaces each markerlight that models in this unit are equipped with and has the following profile:

WEAPON	RANGE	TYPE	S	AP	D
Networked markerlight	36"	Assault 1	-	-	-
Abilities: Markerlights (see *Codex: T'au Empire*).					

ANNIHILATION WARHEADS

Destroyer missiles are rightly named and rightly feared. When fitted with annihilation warheads few foes can stand against their devastating power.

KV128 STORMSURGE model only. When resolving an attack made with a destroyer missile by this model, if it scores a hit do not roll to determine the number of mortal wounds suffered by the target unit; that unit suffers 3 mortal wounds.

ACCELERATED-PHOTON GRENADES

Faced with the devastating charges of the Orks and Tyranids, the Earth caste developed photon grenades that detonate with far greater kinetic energy.

Unit with photon grenades only. This Weapon System replaces each photon grenade that models in this unit are equipped with and has the following profile:

WEAPON	RANGE	TYPE	S	AP	D
Accelerated-photon grenade	12"	Grenade D6	-	-	-
Abilities: This weapon can only target **INFANTRY** units. When resolving an attack made with this weapon, if a hit is scored, do not make a wound roll: instead the target is shocked until the start of your next turn. When resolving an attack made with a melee weapon by a model from a shocked unit, subtract 1 from the hit roll. In addition, shocked units cannot Advance and any charge rolls made for shocked units are halved.					

CROSS-LINKED STABILISER JETS

Hooked in directly to weapon control sub-systems, these sophisticated stabiliser jets enable a battlesuit's weapons to work gyroscopically.

COMMANDER, **XV8 CRISIS BATTLESUITS** or **XV8 CRISIS BODYGUARDS** unit only. When resolving an attack made with a ranged weapon by a model in this unit, re-roll hit rolls of 1 and re-roll wound rolls of 1.

MAGNA RAIL RIFLE

Rare magnetic materials discovered by the T'au of the Fourth Sphere Expansion were used to develop this much-improved version of the rail rifle.

XV88 BROADSIDE BATTLESUITS unit only. This Weapon System replaces each heavy rail rifle models in this unit are equipped with and has the following profile:

WEAPON	RANGE	TYPE	S	AP	D
Magna rail rifle	60"	Heavy 2	9	-4	D6
Abilities: When resolving an attack made with this weapon, a wound roll of 6+ inflicts 1 mortal wound on the target in addition to any other damage. When resolving an attack made with this weapon, a damage roll of 1 or 2 counts as 3 instead.					

AMPLIFIED ION ACCELERATOR

Developed in secrecy over decades, this enormously powerful new weapons system has already proven its worth against the Necrons of the Sautekh Dynasty.

XV104 RIPTIDE BATTLESUIT model only. This Weapon System replaces an ion accelerator and has the following profile:

WEAPON	RANGE	TYPE	S	AP	D
Amplified ion accelerator					
When you choose this weapon to shoot with, select one of the profiles below.					
- Standard	72"	Heavy 6	8	-4	3
- Overcharge	72"	Heavy 6	9	-4	3+D3
Abilities: For each hit roll of 1 made for attacks with this weapon's overcharge profile, the bearer suffers 1 mortal wound after shooting with this weapon.					

HIGH-POWERED INCINERATORS

Fitted with mechanisms to increase pressure and alter nozzle width, these weapons can unleash torrents of deadly flame that are exceptionally powerful at close range.

BATTLESUIT unit only. This Weapon System replaces each flamer that models in this unit are equipped with and has the following profile:

WEAPON	RANGE	TYPE	S	AP	D
High-powered incinerator	8"	Assault D6	4	0	1
Abilities: When resolving an attack made with this weapon, do not make a hit roll: it automatically scores a hit. When resolving an attack made with this weapon against a unit that is within half range, add 1 to the Strength characteristic of this weapon for that attack.					

T'AU EMPIRE STRATAGEMS

If your army is Battle-forged and includes any T'au Empire Detachments (excluding Auxiliary Support Detachments), you have access to the Stratagems shown here, and can spend Command Points to activate them. These reflect the unique strategies used by the forces of the T'au Empire on the battlefield.

SWORN BODYGUARDS
1CP

T'au Empire Stratagem

Crisis Bodyguards rush to the aid of their charge, ready to fight hand-to-hand if necessary to protect them.

Use this Stratagem in the Fight phase, when a <Sept> XV8 Crisis Bodyguards unit from your army is chosen to fight with. Until the end of that phase, when resolving an attack made with a melee weapon by a model in that unit whilst a friendly <Sept> Character unit is within 3" of that model's unit, you can re-roll the hit roll and you can re-roll the wound roll.

AERIAL TARGETING
1CP

T'au Empire Stratagem

Air caste pilots sweep over the battlefield, identifying prime targets for destruction.

Use this Stratagem in your Shooting phase. Select one enemy unit. Until the end of that phase, when resolving an attack made with a ranged weapon by a model from your army against that unit, treat that unit as having one more markerlight counter than it actually has for that attack.

DEADLY AIM
2CP

T'au Empire Stratagem

Careful programming allows Sniper Drones to identify the weakest points in enemy armour.

Use this Stratagem in your Shooting phase, when an MV71 Sniper Drones unit from your army is chosen to shoot with. Until the end of that phase, the Armour Penetration characteristic of longshot pulse rifles models in that unit are equipped with is improved by 1 (e.g. AP 0 becomes AP -1). In addition, until the end of that phase, when resolving an attack made with a longshot pulse rifle by a model in that unit against a unit that is within half range, the Armour Penetration characteristic of that weapon is improved by a further 1 for that attack.

WISDOM OF THE MANY
1CP

T'au Empire Stratagem

The wisest of the T'au Ethereals know how powerful the combined strength of the four castes can be.

Use this Stratagem in your Movement phase. Select one Ethereal unit from your army. Until the end of that phase, that unit can invoke one additional elemental power using its Invocation of the Elements ability, so long as that elemental power has not already been invoked by that unit in that phase.

PULSE ONSLAUGHT
1CP

T'au Empire Stratagem

Where the situation calls for it, Breacher Teams can overcharge their pulse blasters.

Use this Stratagem in your Shooting phase, when a Breacher Team unit from your army is chosen to shoot with. Until the end of that phase, the Range characteristics of the 'Close range' and 'Medium range' profiles for pulse blasters models in that unit are equipped with are increased to 15".

MODULATED WEAPONRY
1CP

T'au Empire Stratagem

The T'au never cease working to maximise the power of their weapon systems, always enhancing their arsenal.

Use this Stratagem in your Shooting phase, when a <Sept> model (other than a Titanic model) from your army is chosen to shoot with. Until the end of that phase, do not roll to determine the Type characteristic of Heavy weapons that model is equipped with; they have their maximum values (e.g. a Heavy D6 weapon makes 6 shots).

RAIN OF FIRE
1CP

T'au Empire Stratagem

As Vespid Stingwings fly around the battlefield, they pour fire on unprotected enemies below.

Use this Stratagem in your Shooting phase, when a Vespid Stingwings unit from your army is chosen to shoot with. Until the end of that phase, when resolving an attack made with a ranged weapon by a model in that unit, if that unit was set up on the battlefield using the Plunge from the Sky ability that turn, you can re-roll the hit roll.

COORDINATED ENGAGEMENT
2CP

T'au Empire Stratagem

T'au combined arms groups are called Hunter Cadres for good reason. Working in close coordination, they hunt and destroy the most dangerous enemy targets.

Use this Stratagem in your Shooting phase. Select one **XV8 Crisis Battlesuits** or **XV8 Crisis Bodyguards** unit from your army, and select one enemy unit. Until the end of that phase, when resolving an attack made by a model in that **XV8 Crisis Battlesuits** or **XV8 Crisis Bodyguards** unit against that enemy unit, treat that enemy unit as having 5 markerlight counters.

AMBUSHING PREDATORS
1CP

T'au Empire Stratagem

Kroot are fierce predators who have learned over millennia the most effective ways to hunt for prey.

Use this Stratagem in your opponent's Charge phase. Select one **Kroot** unit from your army. Until the end of that phase, that unit can perform a Heroic Intervention as if it were a **Character**. In addition, if that unit performs a Heroic Intervention in that phase it can do so if there are any enemy units within 6" of them instead of 3", and when doing so can move up to 6" instead of 3".

SEASONED SNIPER
1CP

T'au Empire Stratagem

Possessed of a calm only veterans wield, the Firesight Marksman singles out priority targets.

Use this Stratagem in your Shooting phase. Select one **Firesight Marksman** model from your army. Until the end of that phase, ranged weapons that model is equipped with can target a **Character** unit even if it is not the closest enemy unit.

HIDDEN HUNTERS
1CP

T'au Empire Stratagem

The Kroot are experts in camouflage and concealment, and utilise cover in ways most would never consider.

Use this Stratagem at the start of your opponent's Shooting phase. Select one **Kroot** unit from your army. Until the end of that phase, when resolving an attack made with a ranged weapon against that unit whilst it is receiving the benefit of cover, subtract 1 from the hit roll and add 1 to the saving throw.

PACK ALPHA
1CP

T'au Empire Stratagem

Some Kroot Shapers earn dominance over their kin through fierce contests or spectacular hunting feats.

Use this Stratagem before the battle. Select one **Kroot Shaper** model from your army. Until the end of the battle, when making an Advance roll or charge roll for a friendly **Kroot** unit within 6" of that model, roll one additional D6 and discard one of the dice.

RAGING BEASTS
1CP

T'au Empire Stratagem

Krootox have immense physical strength, and their riders know how to coax them into terrible rage.

Use this Stratagem when a **Krootox Rider** unit from your army is chosen to fight with in the Fight phase. Until the end of that phase, models in that unit have an Attacks characteristic of 4. In addition, until the end of that phase, the Armour Penetration characteristic of krootox fists models in that unit are equipped with is improved by 2 (e.g. AP 0 becomes AP -2).

POINT-BLANK VOLLEY
1CP

T'au Empire Stratagem

Some T'au perform complex drills in which they train to operate their weapons at extremely close range.

Use this Stratagem at the start of your Shooting phase. Select one <**Sept**> unit from your army. Until the end of that phase, pulse blasters, pulse carbines and pulse rifles models in that unit are equipped with have the Type characteristic of Pistol 2. In addition, until the end of that phase, models in that unit cannot be affected by the Volley Fire ability.

PROMISING PUPIL
1CP

T'au Empire Stratagem

The Fire caste academies imbue in all Fire Warriors the importance of raising up the particularly skilled of their number, for the Greater Good.

Use this Stratagem before the battle, after nominating your Warlord. Select one <**Sept**> **Character** model from your army that does not have a Warlord Trait and determine one Warlord Trait for it; it is regarded as your Warlord for the purposes of that Warlord Trait. Each Warlord Trait in your army must be unique (if randomly generated, re-roll duplicate results).

THE EIGHT

The Eight are the greatest champions of the Farsight Enclaves, led by none other than Commander Farsight himself. This section details who these legendary warriors are, and provides you with rules for using them in your games of Warhammer 40,000.

The Eight take to the battlefield as one, a band of fearless warriors piloting some of the most powerful battlesuits the T'au have ever created. Dynamic and deadly, the Eight act as Farsight's foremost warriors and advisors alike. They fight in perfect concert with a skill that only decades as comrades in arms can forge.

When Commander Farsight goes to war, he does so in swift, dynamic fashion. He is the master of the Mont'ka, the art of identifying a target of opportunity and striking it with maximum force. Farsight leads each assault in person, typically deploying from an overhead Manta Missile Destroyer. Using his jump jets, Farsight descends to his carefully selected targets – for it is vital that the sudden shock and ferocity of the attack put the enemy in immediate peril.

Firing his plasma rifle and crushing enemies beneath the feet of his battlesuit, Commander Farsight lands in a flurry of violence. He swings wide arcs with his sword, the Dawn Blade, an energy-wreathed weapon so potent that it severs ferrocrete as easily as if slicing through water. Before the last of his targets have fallen, Farsight is already in motion, whirling, spinning and chopping until all foes within reach are dead. Activating his jump jets, he leaps into the air, plasma rifle spitting bursts of blue energy that never miss their mark.

Not far behind Commander Farsight come the rest of the Eight, each a whirlwind of devastation. Despite their individual modes of battle the Eight fight flawlessly as a team, each of their number complementing the style and weaponry of the others. Though their choice of armaments and support systems may have changed over time, each warrior has a speciality and way of war that persists and is intimately understood by the others in the team.

Sub-Commander Torchstar sends out sheets of fire even before her battlesuit touches the ground, incinerating those who stand in the Eight's path. Brightsword's twin fusion guns melt away the metal hulls of battle tanks as if made of candle wax. Bravestorm's plasma rifle punches his selected targets off their feet while he closes on a suitable victim for his formidable Onager Gauntlet.

Further from the front, Shas'vre Ob'lotai sends forth steady barrages from his high-yield missile pod, his AI enabling him to simultaneously blast multiple targets across the battlefield. Such long-range tactics are not for Arra'kon, whose battlesuit is bedecked with anti-infantry weapons. With each bounding leap, Arra'kon leaves behind another heap of bodies, the dead falling so thick before his onslaught that they often obscure the ground. Of all the Eight, O'Vesa cuts perhaps the largest swathe of death, his towering XV104 Riptide Battlesuit unleashing prodigious blasts of super-charged energy from its ion accelerator. Shas'o Sha'vastos relays the enemy's movements between delivering volleys from his plasma rifles, allowing the Eight to maintain the relentless pace of their Mont'ka assault and providing the fullest opportunity to bring about the total destruction of their foe.

Despite their rebel status, the Eight are an inspirational embodiment of the T'au warrior spirit, for whom no foe is too great, and no fight so desperate that victory cannot be seized. They are as devoted as any to the supremacy of the T'au race, and it is this conviction that carries Farsight's elite to victory over every foe that stands against them.

HEROES OF THE ENCLAVES

The greatest living legends of the Farsight Enclaves are the Eight. Led by O'Shovah himself, the Eight are warriors beyond compare, the greatest of battlesuit pilots and true masters of the art of war. Farsight could not ask for a more loyal bodyguard.

COMMANDER FARSIGHT

The renegade Fire caste Commander is Shas'o Vior'la Shovah Kais Mont'yr, often shortened to O'Shovah, and even better known as Commander Farsight. Over his unnaturally long lifespan, Farsight has been known by many other names as well, for he was the most exalted of all the protégés of the legendary Commander Puretide. He was also the 'Hero of Vior'la' and 'The Bane of Greenskins' and after he left the Empire, he became known as the 'Great Traitor' or 'He who Renounced the Greater Good'. To the T'au of the Farsight Enclaves, he is their one true leader, a warrior who will take his people to their great destiny.

COMMANDER BRAVESTORM

Commander Bravestorm was entombed in life-support systems after sustaining critical injuries during the battle at Blackthunder Mesa on Dal'yth. Since that fateful day, the scorched and twisted T'au has been confined to a battlesuit, although his core support cocoon has been reinstalled into an XV8-02 Crisis Iridium mantle. Despite his hardships, Bravestorm has lost neither his fervour for the Greater Good, nor his lightning-quick mind. He fights with a battle prowess and bravado that few can equal, for he has passed beyond fear and courted death itself.

COMMANDER BRIGHTSWORD

Few deliver a death blow with such deadly efficiency as Commander Brightsword. With his pair of fusion blasters, Brightsword leads his Rapid Insertion Force from the front, and his war exploits have proven more than worthy. Many famous warriors have previously borne the same name, and the current Brightsword is mindful of the heritage that accompanies the honoured title. In battle, he always chooses the most powerful enemy target to annihilate first, and thus far, none have escaped the blades of energy that form his fusion blades. He has destroyed the most hulking of war engines and monsters, and his aggressive attack style has been modelled upon the tactics of O'Shovah himself.

SHAS'O SHA'VASTOS

Commander Sha'vastos was the first Fire caste warrior to receive a Puretide neurochip. Something went amiss, however, and the prototype chip suffered rapid degeneration. Rather than allow the loyal warrior to suffer a lobotomy, Farsight had him spirited away and placed in stasis until some cure could be discovered. Many decades later, O'Vesa was able to recalibrate the neurochip, and Shas'o Sha'vastos was reawakened. A tactical genius, Commander Sha'vastos leads his cadres to victory after victory, for he always seems to know the enemy's battle plans even before setting foot on the battlefield.

SHAS'O ARRA'KON

Equipped with an XV85 Enforcer battlesuit, and mounting an extensive suite of anti-infantry weapons, Commander Arra'kon can leave even the largest formations of enemy troops in ruins in an instant. Willingly leaving the larger targets to Commander Brightsword, Arra'kon instead seeks out masses of enemy foot soldiers. An analytical warrior, Arra'kon encourages the Eight to review and critique all of their past battles on holo-vid – for it is his constant goal to further hone his battle arts.

BROADSIDE SHAS'VRE OB'LOTAI 9-0

Although it is not known outside of the Eight and their Earth caste attendants, the Broadside battlesuit Ob'lotai 9-0 is not piloted by flesh and blood. Instead, the Broadside is controlled by a late-generation mnemonic AI engram of the original Shas'vre Ob'lotai. Long ago, at the Fire caste training domes, it was Shas'vre Ob'lotai who first taught the piloting arts to the young warrior who would one day become Commander Farsight. Using a velocity tracker and advanced scanfeeds, Ob'lotai 9-0 is a master at supplying the rest of the Eight with deadly accurate supporting fire.

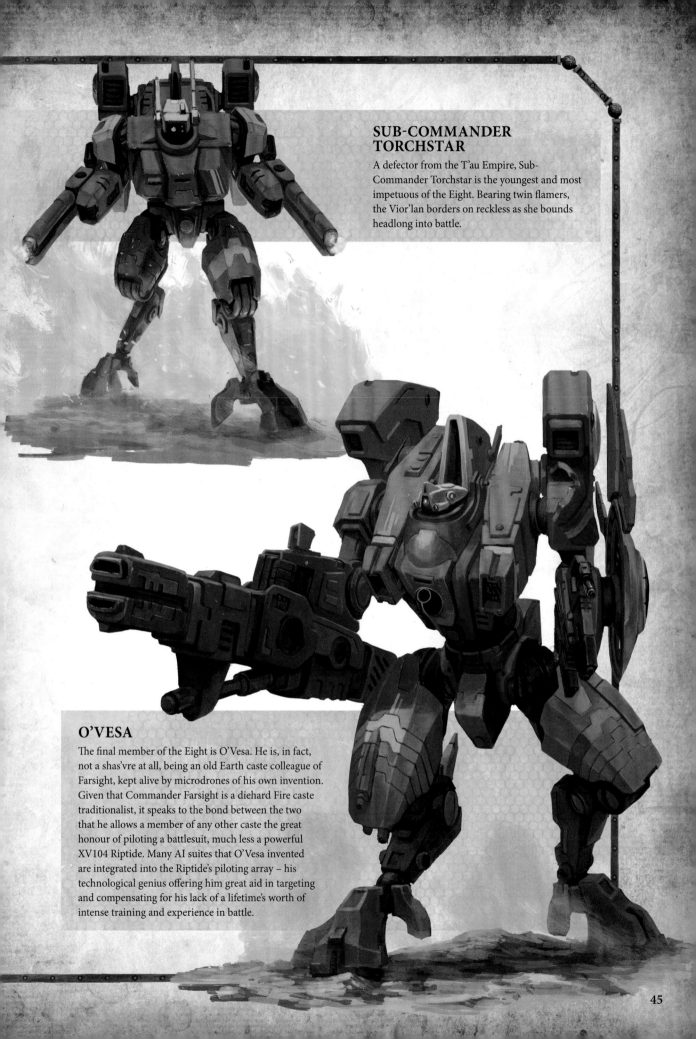

SUB-COMMANDER TORCHSTAR

A defector from the T'au Empire, Sub-Commander Torchstar is the youngest and most impetuous of the Eight. Bearing twin flamers, the Vior'lan borders on reckless as she bounds headlong into battle.

O'VESA

The final member of the Eight is O'Vesa. He is, in fact, not a shas'vre at all, being an old Earth caste colleague of Farsight, kept alive by microdrones of his own invention. Given that Commander Farsight is a diehard Fire caste traditionalist, it speaks to the bond between the two that he allows a member of any other caste the great honour of piloting a battlesuit, much less a powerful XV104 Riptide. Many AI suites that O'Vesa invented are integrated into the Riptide's piloting array – his technological genius offering him great aid in targeting and compensating for his lack of a lifetime's worth of intense training and experience in battle.

USING THE EIGHT IN BATTLE

This section details the rules that allow you to field the Eight in your battles, including the datasheet for these mighty heroes and the rules required to include them in your army. You will also find a summary of the weapons they wield here, along with abilities that are common to several of their number.

Including the Eight in Your Army

The datasheet for the Eight can be found on pages 48-49. If your army is Battle-forged, you can only include this datasheet in a Super-heavy Auxiliary Detachment; if you do the Command Benefits of that Detachment are changed to '-3 Command Points', and you cannot give any model in your army a Signature System. This is to take account of the Signature Systems that are always equipped on various members of the Eight (effectively, the Emergency Dispensation Stratagem has automatically been used to give the Eight the various Signature Systems they require).

Matched Play Rules

Matched Play Rules that restrict the number of **Commander** units allowed in each Detachment do not apply to the Eight's Detachment.

Commander Farsight

If you include the Eight in your army then you cannot also include the **Commander Farsight** datasheet from *Codex: T'au Empire*. Furthermore, if you include the Eight in your army, **Commander Farsight** must be your army's Warlord, and he has the following Warlord Trait:

Hero of the Enclaves: This Warlord can perform a Heroic Intervention if there are any enemy units within 6" of them instead of 3", and when doing so can move up to 6" instead of 3". If this Warlord makes a charge move, is charged or performs a Heroic Intervention, until the end of the turn, when resolving an attack made by this Warlord, you can re-roll the hit roll.

Points Value

If you are playing a matched play game, or a game that uses a points limit, then the points value for the Eight can be found below. Simply add this to the cost of your other models and the wargear they are equipped with to determine your army's total points value.

THE EIGHT		
UNIT	MODELS PER UNIT	POINTS PER UNIT (Including wargear)
The Eight	8 Characters 14 Drones	1120

Abilities

The following abilities apply to several of the Eight:

Master of War

Once per battle, at the start of your turn, a single **Farsight Enclaves Commander** unit from your army can declare either Kauyon or Mont'ka:

Kauyon: In a turn in which a **Farsight Enclaves Commander** unit from your army declared Kauyon, at the start of your Movement phase you can select any friendly **Farsight Enclaves** units within 6" of that unit. Until the end of that turn, the selected units cannot move for any reason, but when resolving an attack made by a model in any of those units you can re-roll the hit roll.

Mont'ka: In a turn in which a **Farsight Enclaves Commander** unit from your army declared Mont'ka, at the start of your Movement phase you can select any friendly **Farsight Enclaves** units within 6" of that unit. Until the end of that turn, the selected units can shoot as if they did not move this turn.

Unless stated otherwise, you can only use the Master of War ability once per battle, irrespective of how many models in your army have this ability.

Sept Tenet

If your army is Battle-forged, all models in the Eight's Detachment gain the following Sept Tenet:

Devastating Counter-strike: When resolving an attack made with a ranged weapon by a model with this tenet against a unit within 6", you can re-roll a wound roll of 1.

Enclave Drone Support

When a **Character** from the Eight is set up on the battlefield, any accompanying **Drone** models are set up in unit coherency with it. From that point onwards, those **Drone** models are treated as a separate unit with the HQ Battlefield Role, and are considered to have a Power Rating of 0.

Saviour Protocols

When resolving an attack made against a **Farsight Enclaves Infantry** or **Farsight Enclaves Battlesuit** unit whilst that unit is within 3" of a friendly **Farsight Enclaves Drones** unit, if the wound roll is successful, you can roll one D6; on a 2+ that **Drones** unit suffers a mortal wound and the attack sequence ends.

WEAPONS

WEAPON	RANGE	TYPE	S	AP	D	ABILITIES
Airbursting fragmentation projector	18"	Assault D6	4	0	1	This weapon can target units that are not visible to the bearer.
Cyclic ion blaster	When you choose this weapon to shoot with, select one of the profiles below.					
- Standard	18"	Assault 3	7	-1	1	-
- Overcharge	18"	Assault 3	8	-1	D3	For each hit roll of 1 made for attacks with this weapon, the bearer suffers 1 mortal wound after shooting with this weapon.
Flamer	8"	Assault D6	4	0	1	When resolving an attack made with this weapon, do not make a hit roll: it automatically scores a hit.
Fusion Blades (ranged)	18"	Assault 2	8	-4	D6	When resolving an attack made with this weapon against a unit that is within half range, roll one additional D6 when inflicting damage with it and discard one of the dice.
Fusion blaster	18"	Assault 1	8	-4	D6	When resolving an attack made with this weapon against a unit that is within half range, roll one additional D6 when inflicting damage with it and discard one of the dice.
High-intensity plasma rifle	30"	Rapid Fire 1	6	-4	2	-
High-yield missile pod	36"	Heavy 4	7	-1	D3	-
Ion accelerator	When you choose this weapon to shoot with, select one of the profiles below.					
- Standard	72"	Heavy D6	8	-3	D3	-
- Overcharge	72"	Heavy D6	9	-3	3	For each hit roll of 1 made for attacks with this weapon, the bearer suffers 1 mortal wound after shooting with this weapon.
Markerlight	36"	Heavy 1	-	-	-	Markerlights (see *Codex: T'au Empire*)
Missile pod	36"	Assault 2	7	-1	D3	-
Plasma rifle	24"	Rapid Fire 1	6	-3	1	-
Pulse carbine	18"	Assault 2	5	0	1	-
Seeker missile	72"	Heavy 1	8	-2	D6	The bearer can only shoot with each seeker missile it is equipped with once per battle. When resolving an attack made with this weapon, only an unmodified hit roll of 6 scores a hit.
Smart missile system	30"	Heavy 4	5	0	1	This weapon can target units that are not visible to the bearer. When resolving an attack made with this weapon, the target does not receive the benefit of cover.
Dawn Blade	Melee	Melee	+3	-4	D3	-
Fusion Blades (melee)	Melee	Melee	8	-4	D6	When the bearer fights, it makes 2 additional attacks with this weapon and no more than 2 attacks can be made with this weapon.
Onager Gauntlet	Melee	Melee	10	-4	D6	When the bearer fights, it makes 1 additional attack with this weapon and no more than 1 attack can be made with this weapon.

SUPPORT SYSTEMS

SYSTEM	EFFECT
Advanced targeting system	When resolving an attack made with a weapon by a model that has an advanced targeting system, improve the Armour Penetration characteristic of that weapon by 1 for that attack (e.g. AP 0 becomes AP -1).
Counterfire defence system	When resolving an Overwatch attack made by a model that has a counterfire defence system, you can re-roll the hit roll.
Drone controller	When resolving an attack made by a model from a **FARSIGHT ENCLAVES DRONE** unit within 6" of any friendly models that have a drone controller, add 1 to the hit roll.
Early warning override	If any enemy units are set up on the battlefield as reinforcements within 12" of a model from your army that has an early warning override, at the end of the phase that model can shoot at one of those units as if it were your Shooting phase. When resolving each of those attacks, subtract 1 from the hit roll.
Shield generator	Models that have a shield generator have a 4+ invulnerable save. A XV104 **RIPTIDE BATTLESUIT** model cannot have a shield generator.
Target lock	Models that have a target lock do not suffer the penalty for moving and firing Heavy weapons or for Advancing and firing Assault weapons. Models that have a target lock can shoot Rapid Fire weapons they are equipped with even if they Advanced, but when resolving such an attack by an **INFANTRY** model, subtract 1 from the hit roll.
Velocity tracker	When resolving an attack made with a ranged weapon by a model that has a velocity tracker against a unit that can **FLY**, add 1 to the hit roll.

THE EIGHT

DAMAGE			
Some of O'Vesa's characteristics change as he suffers damage, as shown below:			
REMAINING W	M	BS	A
7-14+	12"	4+	4
4-6	8"	5+	3
1-3	4"	5+	2

NAME	M	WS	BS	S	T	W	A	Ld	Sv
Commander Farsight	8"	2+	2+	5	5	6	4	9	3+
Commander Brightsword	8"	3+	2+	5	5	5	4	9	3+
Commander Bravestorm	8"	3+	2+	5	5	5	4	9	2+
Shas'o Sha'vastos	8"	3+	2+	5	5	5	4	9	3+
Shas'o Arra'kon	8"	3+	2+	5	5	6	4	9	3+
Sub-Commander Torchstar	8"	3+	2+	5	5	5	4	9	3+
Broadside Shas'vre Ob'lotai 9-0	5"	5+	4+	5	5	6	3	8	2+
O'Vesa	*	6+	*	6	7	14	*	8	2+
MV1 Gun Drone	8"	5+	5+	3	4	1	1	6	4+
MV4 Shield Drone	8"	5+	5+	3	4	1	1	6	4+
MV7 Marker Drone	8"	5+	5+	3	4	1	1	6	4+
MV8 Missile Drone	8"	5+	5+	3	4	1	1	6	4+
MV84 Shielded Missile Drone	12"	5+	5+	4	4	1	1	6	4+

You can only include one of this unit in your army. This unit contains the following eight characters and their accompanying Drones:
- Commander Farsight is a single model equipped with: high-intensity plasma rifle; Dawn Blade. It has a shield generator.
- Commander Brightsword is a single model equipped with: Fusion Blades. It has a counterfire defence system and a target lock. It is accompanied by 2 MV4 Shield Drones.
- Commander Bravestorm is a single model equipped with: flamer; plasma rifle; Onager Gauntlet. It has an advanced targeting system and a shield generator. It is accompanied by 2 MV1 Gun Drones, each equipped with: 2 pulse carbines.
- Shas'o Sha'vastos is a single model equipped with: flamer; plasma rifle. It has a drone controller and a shield generator. It is accompanied by 2 MV1 Gun Drones, each equipped with: 2 pulse carbines.
- Shas'o Arra'kon is a single model equipped with: airbursting fragmentation projector; cyclic ion blaster; plasma rifle. It has a counterfire defence system. It is accompanied by 2 MV1 Gun Drones, each equipped with: 2 pulse carbines.
- Sub-Commander Torchstar is a single model equipped with: 2 flamers. It has an advanced targeting system and a drone controller. It is accompanied by 2 MV7 Marker Drones, each equipped with: markerlight.
- Broadside Shas'vre Ob'lotai 9-0 is a single model equipped with: 2 high-yield missile pods; seeker missile; 2 smart missile systems. It has a velocity tracker. It is accompanied by 2 MV8 Missile Drones, each equipped with: missile pod.
- O'Vesa is a single model equipped with: 2 fusion blasters; ion accelerator. It has an early warning override and a target lock. It is accompanied by 2 MV84 Shielded Missile Drones, each equipped with: missile pod.

ABILITIES	**For the Greater Good:** When a unit declares a charge against a unit from your army within 6" of this unit, this unit can fire Overwatch at the charging unit. If it does, this unit cannot fire Overwatch again this turn.
	Accompanying Drones: During deployment, every model in this unit must be set up at the same time, though they do not need to be set up in unit coherency (see the Enclave Drone Support ability on page 46 for details on how to place a model's accompanying Drone models). From that point onwards, each **CHARACTER** model is treated as a separate unit and is considered to have a Power Rating of 7.
	Manta Drop: During deployment, with the exception of O'Vesa, you can set up **CHARACTER** models (and any accompanying Drone models) in this unit in a Manta hold instead of setting them up on the battlefield. If you do, at the end of one of your Movement phases you can set up those **CHARACTER** models anywhere on the battlefield that is more than 9" away from any enemy models.
ABILITIES (FARSIGHT)	**Master of War** (see *Codex: T'au Empire*)
	Genius of Mont'ka: Once per battle, this model can declare Mont'ka even if Kauyon or Mont'ka has already been declared. Mont'ka and Kauyon cannot both be declared in the same turn.
	Way of the Short Blade: Re-roll hit rolls of 1 for attacks made with melee weapons by models in friendly **FARSIGHT ENCLAVES** units whilst their unit is within 6" of this model. Re-roll hit rolls of 1 for attacks made with ranged weapons by models in friendly **FARSIGHT ENCLAVES** units against an **ORK** unit whilst their unit is within 6" of this model.

ABILITIES (BRIGHTSWORD)	Master of War (see *Codex: T'au Empire*)
	Warscaper Drones: Subtract 2 from charge rolls made for enemy units if they are within 12" of any of this model's accompanying MV4 Shield Drone models when the roll is made.
ABILITIES (BRAVESTORM)	Master of War (see *Codex: T'au Empire*)
	Advanced Support Cocoon: When this model would lose a wound, roll one D6; on a 6 that wound is not lost.
ABILITIES (SHA'VASTOS)	Master of War (see *Codex: T'au Empire*)
	Puretide Engram Neurochip: Once per battle, when resolving an attack made by a friendly FARSIGHT ENCLAVES model within 6" of this model, you can re-roll the hit roll, wound roll or damage roll. Whilst this model is on the battlefield, you can roll one D6 each time you or your opponent use a Stratagem; on a 6 you gain 1 Command Point. You can only gain 1 Command Point per battle round from this ability.
ABILITIES (ARRA'KON)	Master of War (see *Codex: T'au Empire*)
	Repulsor Impact Field: After an enemy unit finishes a charge move within 1" of this model, roll one D6; on a 2+, that enemy unit suffers 1 mortal wound.
ABILITIES (TORCHSTAR)	Master of War (see *Codex: T'au Empire*)
	Neuroweb System Jammer: Enemy units that are set up on the battlefield as reinforcements cannot be set up within 12" of this model. When resolving an attack made with a ranged weapon against this model's unit, subtract 1 from the hit roll.
ABILITIES (OB'LOTAI 9-0)	**No Longer Flesh and Blood:** When resolving an attack made with a weapon against this model, subtract 1 from the Damage characteristic of that weapon (to a minimum of 1) for that attack.
	Advanced Scan Feeds: This model does not suffer the penalty for moving and firing Heavy weapons.
ABILITIES (O'VESA)	**Riptide Shield Generator:** This model has a 5+ invulnerable save.
	Earth Caste Pilot Array: When resolving an attack made with a ranged weapon by this model, you can re-roll a hit roll of 1. When this model would lose a wound as a result of its Nova Reactor ability, roll one D6; on a 4+ that wound is not lost.
	Nova Reactor: In your Movement phase you can choose to use this model's Nova Reactor. If you do, this model suffers 1 mortal wound and you can select one of the following effects to last until the start of your next turn: • **Nova Shield:** This model has a 3+ invulnerable save. • **Boost:** In your Charge phase, if this model does not make a charge move, it can make a move of 2D6" as if it were your Movement phase. • **Nova-charge:** Ion accelerators this model is equipped with have a Type characteristic of Heavy 6.
ABILITIES (DRONES)	**Saviour Protocols, Enclave Drone Support** (pg 46)
	Shield Generator: MV4 Shield Drone and MV84 Shielded Missile Drone models have a 4+ invulnerable save. When an MV4 Shield Drone or MV84 Shielded Missile Drone model would lose a wound, roll one D6; on a 5+ that wound is not lost.
FACTION KEYWORDS	T'AU EMPIRE, FARSIGHT ENCLAVES
KEYWORDS (FARSIGHT)	BATTLESUIT, CHARACTER, JET PACK, FLY, COMMANDER, FARSIGHT
KEYWORDS (BRIGHTSWORD)	BATTLESUIT, CHARACTER, XV8 CRISIS, JET PACK, FLY, COMMANDER, BRIGHTSWORD
KEYWORDS (BRAVESTORM)	BATTLESUIT, CHARACTER, XV8 CRISIS, JET PACK, FLY, COMMANDER, BRAVESTORM
KEYWORDS (SHA'VASTOS)	BATTLESUIT, CHARACTER, XV8 CRISIS, JET PACK, FLY, COMMANDER, SHAS'O SHA'VASTOS
KEYWORDS (ARRA'KON)	BATTLESUIT, CHARACTER, XV85 ENFORCER, JET PACK, FLY, COMMANDER, SHAS'O ARRA'KON
KEYWORDS (TORCHSTAR)	BATTLESUIT, CHARACTER, XV8 CRISIS, JET PACK, FLY, COMMANDER, TORCHSTAR
KEYWORDS (OB'LOTAI 9-0)	BATTLESUIT, CHARACTER, XV88 BROADSIDE, SHAS'VRE OB'LOTAI 9-0
KEYWORDS (O'VESA)	BATTLESUIT, CHARACTER, MONSTER, JET PACK, FLY, XV104 RIPTIDE, O'VESA
KEYWORDS (GUN, SHIELD AND MARKER DRONES)	DRONE, FLY, TACTICAL DRONES
KEYWORDS (MISSILE DRONES)	DRONE, FLY, MV8 MISSILE DRONES
KEYWORDS (SHIELDED MISSILE DRONES)	DRONE, FLY, MV84 SHIELDED MISSILE DRONES

FORCES OF THE ENCLAVES

This section contains new and updated rules for the Farsight Enclaves subfaction from *Codex: T'au Empire*, including Stratagems, Relics, Warlord Traits and Tactical Objectives.

MATCHED PLAY RULE: COMMANDERS

If you are playing a matched play game with a Battle-forged army, you can include no more than two FARSIGHT ENCLAVES COMMANDER units in each Detachment.

ABILITIES

All FARSIGHT ENCLAVES units in *Codex: T'au Empire* gain the Aggressive Footing ability:

AGGRESSIVE FOOTING

When resolving an attack made with a ranged weapon by a model in this unit against an enemy unit within 12", treat that enemy unit as having one more markerlight counter than it actually has.

'Some say that perfection is the enemy of the good. They speak nonsense. Such apathetic thinking is what turns that which is good into bad. We should never cease our striving for greatness, never halt our pursuit of bettering ourselves. Anything else is nothing but stagnation, and I have seen enough of the galaxy to know that to stagnate is to wither and die in shameful ignominy.'

- Shas'o Arra'kon

FARSIGHT ENCLAVES STRATAGEMS

If your army is Battle-forged and includes any Farsight Enclaves Detachments (excluding Auxiliary Support Detachments), you have access to the Stratagems shown here, and can spend Command Points to activate them. When one of these Stratagems refers to a unit from your army, that unit must also be from a Farsight Enclaves Detachment.

VETERAN CADRE
1/2CP

Farsight Enclaves Stratagem
Many of Farsight's followers have fought in countless battles against myriad foes.

Use this Stratagem before the battle. Select one XV8 CRISIS BATTLESUITS or XV8 CRISIS BODYGUARDS unit from your army that contains 3 models for 1 Command Point or one XV8 CRISIS BATTLESUITS or XV8 CRISIS BODYGUARDS unit from your army that contains 4 or more models for 2 Command Points. Models in that unit have a Weapon Skill characteristic of 4+ and a Ballistic Skill characteristic of 3+. You can only use this Stratagem once per battle.

DEFENCE IN NUMBERS
2CP

Farsight Enclaves Stratagem
Farsight ensures that damaged battlesuits are rotated out of combat to preserve his warriors' lives.

Use this Stratagem in the Fight phase or your opponent's Shooting phase, when an XV8 CRISIS BATTLESUITS or XV8 CRISIS BODYGUARDS unit from your army is chosen as the target for an attack. Until the end of that phase, when a model in that unit would lose a wound, roll one D6; on a 5+ that wound is not lost.

FURIOUS ASSAULT
1CP

Farsight Enclaves Stratagem
Using the powerful thrusters of their huge battlesuits, Farsight's warriors slam into the fray.

Use this Stratagem in your Charge phase, when a JET PACK unit from your army finishes a charge move. For each model in that unit, you can select one enemy unit within 1" of that model and roll one D6; on a 3+ that enemy unit suffers 1 mortal wound.

FOCUSED FURY
1CP

Farsight Enclaves Stratagem
T'au officers are often equipped with advanced targeting equipment that identifies weak points in enemy defences.

Use this Stratagem in your Shooting phase, when a CHARACTER model from your army is chosen to shoot with. Until the end of that phase, when resolving an attack made by that model, you can re-roll the wound roll.

DANGER CLOSE
1CP

Farsight Enclaves Stratagem
Fire Warrior teams of the Farsight Enclaves receive extensive training in close-quarters combat.

Use this Stratagem in your Shooting phase, when a BREACHER TEAM or STRIKE TEAM unit from your army is chosen to shoot with. Until the end of that phase, when resolving an attack made with a ranged weapon by a model in that unit against an enemy unit within 12", you can re-roll the wound roll.

FIRESTORM
1CP

Farsight Enclaves Stratagem
In a terrific onslaught, Farsight Enclave flyers rain hell upon their foes, saturating them with heavy fire.

Use this Stratagem at the end of your Movement phase. Select up to three T'AU EMPIRE units with the Flyer Battlefield Role from your army. This Stratagem costs 1 additional Command Point for each selected unit. Roll one D6 for each enemy unit within 3" of any of those selected units. On a 4+ that enemy unit suffers D3 mortal wounds.

'Each must find their own way. If those in our heartland had witnessed the savageries of the void as have we, they would know this. Each of the great starfarers turn their hands against the other; none will join their strength together just to see their ancient enemies prosper. Neither should we.'

- Commander Farsight

ENCLAVE RELICS

If your army is led by a Farsight Enclaves Warlord, you can give one of the following Enclave Relics to a Farsight Enclaves **Character** model from your army instead of giving them a Signature System from *Codex: T'au Empire*. Named characters cannot be given any of the following Enclave Relics.

The Mirrorcodex

After the Damocles Crusade, Farsight applied his genius to unravelling the Imperium's war doctrine, codifying the main tenets of both the Tactica Imperialis and the Codex Astartes. Farsight attempts the same with every alien species he encounters, incorporating what he learns into his Da'thle'vral, or 'Mirrorcodex'.

When resolving an attack made by a model with this Relic against a unit that is within 18", you can re-roll the hit roll.

Talisman of Arthas Moloch

The artefact world of Arthas Moloch was little more than a devastated wasteland when the Farsight Expedition arrived. Yet the T'au recovered a number of strange relics there, amongst them a hexagrammatic talisman. Farsight has seen first hand that this arcane object protects its wearer and those around them from baleful energies, though neither he nor his advisors have the faintest idea of how it does so.

A model with this Relic has a 5+ invulnerable save. A model with this Relic can attempt to resist one psychic power in your opponent's Psychic phase in the same manner as a **Psyker** by taking a Deny the Witch test, if that model is within 24" of the enemy model manifesting that psychic power.

Seismic Fibrillator Node

On his adopted home planet of Vior'los, O'Shovah bested the Ork Warlord Grog by turning the elements against him. Instrumental in these victories was the Seismic Fibrillator Node, an invention of Earth caste scientist O'Vesa. This disc-like device emits resonant frequencies of such power that they cause localised earth tremors of great magnitude.

Once per battle, at the start of your opponent's turn, you can choose to activate this Relic. If you do, until the end of that turn, when a model starts or ends a move within 6" of a model with this Relic, roll one D6; on a 1 that model's unit suffers 1 mortal wound.

WARLORD TRAITS

If a Farsight Enclaves **Character** model is your Warlord, you can use the Warlord Traits table below to determine what Warlord Trait they have instead of using the Warlord Traits table from *Codex: T'au Empire*. You can either roll one D3 to randomly generate one, or you can select one.

1 BLOODED THROUGH WAR

Those Commanders who have led a multitude of bloody campaigns have thoroughly earned the trust of their warriors. Such is this bond of loyalty that their troops will courageously follow them into the harshest of battles.

When a Morale test is taken for a friendly **Farsight Enclaves** unit with the Bonding Knife Ritual ability whilst within 12" of this Warlord, it is automatically passed on a roll of 4+, instead of 6.

2 AGGRESSIVE TACTICIAN

This warlord is always on the attack, striking hard again and again with their forces until the enemy is entirely destroyed. They give no respite and show no mercy, seeing both as weakness.

COMMANDER model only. When this Warlord declares Mont'ka, it affects friendly **Farsight Enclaves** units within 12" of this Warlord, instead of within 6".

3 MASTER OF THE KILLING BLOW

This warlord knows that cutting the head from the snake is a sound battlefield tactic in any war, and they pursue enemy commanders and warlords relentlessly. Once they are successful in their hunt, their enemies' forces collapse into disarray and are easy prey.

When resolving an attack made by this Warlord against a **CHARACTER** unit, you can re-roll the hit roll.

FARSIGHT ENCLAVES TACTICAL OBJECTIVES

These Tactical Objectives are for use in Maelstrom of War missions to represent the strategies and tactics of the Farsight Enclaves on the battlefield.

If your army is led by a Farsight Enclaves Warlord, these Tactical Objectives replace the Capture and Control Tactical Objectives (numbers 11-16) in the *Warhammer 40,000* rulebook. If a mission uses Tactical Objectives, players use the normal rules for using Tactical Objectives with the following exception: when a Farsight Enclaves player generates a Capture and Control objective (numbers 11-16), they instead generate the corresponding Farsight Enclaves Tactical Objective, as shown below. Other Tactical Objectives (numbers 21-66) are generated normally.

D66	TACTICAL OBJECTIVE
11	Target of Opportunity
12	Directed Firepower
13	Critical Takeover
14	Aggressive Infiltration
15	Order of Execution
16	Calculated Assassination

11 — TARGET OF OPPORTUNITY

Delivered at the right time, the death of certain foes can determine the outcome of an entire war.

Declare that you are going to attempt to achieve this objective at the start of any of your turns, and then pick three enemy units. Score 3 victory points if two or more of those enemy units were destroyed this turn by units from your army. Score an additional D3 victory points if all three of those enemy units were destroyed this turn by units from your army.

Farsight Enclaves

12 — DIRECTED FIREPOWER

Close with the enemy. Look into their eyes. Know that you are their death, and the last thing they will see.

Score 1 victory point if at least one enemy unit was destroyed by a unit from your army this turn whilst they were within 12" of that unit.

Farsight Enclaves

13 — CRITICAL TAKEOVER

Our claim is to the entirety of the galaxy. None can take from us what is rightfully ours.

Score D3 victory points if at least one enemy unit was destroyed this turn by a unit from your army whilst that enemy unit was within 3" of an objective marker, and you control that objective marker.

Farsight Enclaves

14 — AGGRESSIVE INFILTRATION

Push the enemy back to where they came from. Do not hesitate, do not slow down. Harry them until the last, give them no opportunity to regroup.

Score D3 victory points if at least one enemy unit was destroyed this turn by a unit from your army that is wholly within the enemy deployment zone.

Farsight Enclaves

15 — ORDER OF EXECUTION

Our enemies must fall in the order best suited to victory. With each kill will the battle grow easier.

Score 1 victory point if at least one enemy unit was destroyed by the first unit you chose to shoot with in the Shooting phase this turn.

Farsight Enclaves

16 — CALCULATED ASSASSINATION

Without their leaders, our enemies will fall into disorder, and our victory will follow.

Score 1 victory point if at least one enemy CHARACTER unit was destroyed this turn by a unit from your army.

Farsight Enclaves

ASTRA MILITARUM

'The marching ranks of infantry. The rumbling columns of tanks. Beautiful music all. But when they open fire… such harmonies and symphonies move the soul to tears.'

- Field Marshal Kleiss Ivanek, 5th Riatov Grand Army Group

HAMMER OF THE IMPERIUM

This section contains new and updated rules for the Astra Militarum, including new Stratagems, rules for creating custom Regimental Doctrines and using Tank Aces, and a supplement for the Militarum Tempestus. The section also includes a name generator for adding extra character to your army.

This section is a supplement to *Codex: Astra Militarum* – you will need a copy of that book to use the rules in this section.

Name Generator

The troops of the Astra Militarum are recruited from almost every world in the Imperium, giving you boundless choice in how to name your soldiers. On the opposite page you will find a name generator for your Astra Militarum warriors, allowing you to further personalise units from your army.

Regimental Doctrines

Pages 58-59 present rules for creating your own Regimental Doctrines. These comprise a selection of abilities that can be combined to represent the fighting styles of a regiment of your own devising, or a regiment from our publications that is not currently represented by a Regimental Doctrine in *Codex: Astra Militarum.*

Tank Aces

The Astra Militarum is a highly mechanised force, and amongst its vast numbers of tank crews are many experienced veterans. Pages 60-61 present rules for upgrading the tanks in your army to represent these skilled warriors.

Stratagems

Pages 62-63 present a number of new Stratagems that can be used by **ASTRA MILITARUM** Detachments in addition to those found in *Codex: Astra Militarum*. These bring a new range of tactical options to the loyal servants of the Emperor.

The Ordo Tempestus

Pages 64-69 present a dedicated supplement allowing you to field the elite special forces of the Militarum Tempestus, including Regimental Doctrines, Stratagems, Warlord Traits and Relics.

'Traitor, mutant, alien, heretic, they're all the same to me. Haven't seen one yet that can stand up to the tracks of a Leman Russ, and I've still got to clean off what's left of them when the fighting's done regardless.'

- *Sergeant Vance Eshmet, 4th Euthenian Hussars*

ASTRA MILITARUM NAME GENERATOR

If you wish to create a name for one of your Astra Militarum troopers, you can roll a D66 and consult one of the tables below, or pick a name that inspires you. To roll a D66, simply roll two D6, one after the other – the first represents tens and the second represents digits, giving you a result between 11 and 66.

CADIAN NAMES		CATACHAN NAMES		VALHALLAN NAMES		VOSTROYAN NAMES	
D66	**TROOPER**	**D66**	**TROOPER**	**D66**	**TROOPER**	**D66**	**TROOPER**
11	Jens	11	Gunnarsen	11	Vensk	11	Davoren
12	Karsk	12	Harker	12	Skarrsen	12	Vanya
13	Hekler	13	Grytt	13	Chernov	13	Sinissa
14	Reeve	14	'Snake' Vandien	14	Dushenko	14	Senkaa
15	Pavlo	15	Greiss	15	Rynsk	15	Ilyas
16	Hektor	16	Stryker	16	Gorska	16	Rasuul
21	Nils	21	Storm	21	Varence	21	Roshtam
22	Thenmann	22	Lance	22	Nyska	22	Solfiya
23	Kyser	23	'Crazy' Winters	23	Putran	23	Culpan
24	Erlen	24	Cage	24	Dorff	24	Xabirra
25	Raphe	25	Hammer	25	Tyvosk	25	Matis
26	Creed	26	Cobra	26	Polanski	26	Dovydas
31	Lasko	31	'Hardhead' Jackson	31	Drekoff	31	Darius
32	Ackerman	32	'Stonefist' Kage	32	Vorn	32	Valdemar
33	Mattias	33	'Boss' Stransky	33	Hapscheldt	33	Valter
34	Mortens	34	'Bomber' Johnson	34	Olof	34	Andris
35	Dansk	35	Jacksen	35	Trevinska	35	Kriss
36	Feodor	36	Marshall	36	Schonnen	36	Olvegg
41	Tomas	41	'Fangs' Lorson	41	Kleiss	41	Vygand
42	Kolson	42	'Cold-eye' McKay	42	Borys	42	Ethsmar
43	Vance	43	Wolf	43	Ivanek	43	Damir
44	Pask	44	'Shiv' Frost	44	Smirnek	44	Dalibor
45	Niems	45	Brent	45	Kuzentsev	45	Jarek
46	Gryf	46	'Ironheart' McKillen	46	Vasilesnev	46	Gavrick
51	Willem	51	'Killer' Crowe	51	Petravitch	51	Serhii
52	Sonnen	52	'Wildman' Weiss	52	Skolov	52	Lazlo
53	Ekhter	53	'Ice' Creek	53	Fedorev	53	Bohdan
54	Farestein	54	Dane	54	Morazev	54	Aljor
55	Dekker	55	Steeljaw	55	Volko	55	Emelian
56	Graf	56	Dransky	56	Lebesnev	56	Vaslek
61	Arvans	61	'Slim' Hasker	61	Egoryn	61	Konstan
62	Viers	62	Mason	62	Pavlek	62	Djozep
63	Kolm	63	Hawks	63	Kozlev	63	Ostap
64	Bask	64	Axel	64	Stepanovicz	64	Jesaul
65	Vesker	65	Carver	65	Nikoli	65	Yermak
66	Pavlo	66	Payne	66	Orlakev	66	Stratiz

REGIMENTAL DOCTRINES

Every planet in the Imperium raises regiments for the Astra Militarum. Each world's troops have their own distinct traditions, training regimes, tactics and preferred methods of waging war. Even regiments from the same planet can vary, and the rules below will help you develop your own unique fighting force.

Codex: Astra Militarum describes how the <Regiment> keyword can be substituted with the name of your chosen regiment, as well as describing the abilities that units in **Astra Militarum** Detachments gain. One of these abilities is Regimental Doctrines. If your chosen regiment does not have an associated Regimental Doctrine in *Codex: Astra Militarum*, you can create its Regimental Doctrine by selecting two rules from the following list:

Gunnery Experts

The troops of some Astra Militarum armoured regiments spend countless weeks drilling with their vehicles' weapons, ensuring every reload is swift and precise even when the crew are under immense pressure.

When you roll to determine the Type characteristic of any weapon a **Vehicle** model with this doctrine is equipped with, you can re-roll one of the dice.

Spotter Details

Drawing on extensive training, the gunners and spotters of this regiment form extremely effective partnerships that can have devastating consequences for the enemy.

Add 6" to the Range characteristic of Heavy weapons with a range of at least 24" that models with this doctrine are equipped with.

Disciplined Shooters

There are few skills more explicitly soldierly than that of marksmanship. Having spent countless hours on ranges, the warriors of this regiment have honed their skills with all manner of weapons to ensure controlled fire even in the harshest battlefield conditions. Remaining calm under immense pressure, these soldiers are capable of pouring vast quantities of accurate fire on enemies that draw close enough, demonstrating impressive clarity of thought.

When an **Infantry** model with this doctrine shoots with a Rapid Fire weapon against a unit that is within 18", double the number of attacks that weapon makes, rather than following the normal rules for Rapid Fire weapons.

Fire from the Hip

Some regiments develop sophisticated mobile warfare tactics, specialising in rapid assaults and flexible defences. Their soldiers learn to fire accurately on the move, and are able to pour suppressing fire on the enemy even whilst rushing from cover to cover.

Infantry models with this doctrine can shoot Rapid Fire weapons they are equipped with even if they Advanced, but when resolving such an attack, subtract 1 from the hit roll.

Combined Auspex

The vehicles of this regiment share auspex readings to best track and target charging enemies, protecting their comrades from harm.

When resolving an Overwatch attack made by a <Regiment> **Vehicle** model with this doctrine whilst within 3" of another friendly <Regiment> **Vehicle** unit, a hit roll of 5+ scores a hit.

Agile Warriors

The soldier is the most deadly weapon of all in the eyes of some Astra Militarum regiments, whose rigorous training regimens place an emphasis on forward assault.

When an **Infantry** unit with this doctrine Advances, you can re-roll the Advance roll.

Pyromaniacs

There are few better ways of scouring a foe from a world than with torrents of burning promethium. Some regiments embrace this fact, mastering the use of flamer weapons and upgrading them with increased power.

When resolving an attack made with a flamer, heavy flamer or twin heavy flamer by a model with this doctrine, you can re-roll a wound roll of 1.

Wilderness Survivors

Many peoples of the Imperium dwell in harsh wildlands, becoming experts in tracking and camouflage. The Astra Militarum puts these hard-earned skills to great use.

When resolving an attack made with a ranged weapon against an **Infantry** unit with this doctrine, if that unit did not Advance in its previous Movement phase, it is treated as receiving the benefit of cover to its saving throws.

Jury-rigged Repairs

Last minute vehicle tune-ups before a battle can stop a track breaking or a weapon misfiring in combat, but the ability to repair damage mid-battle can be the difference between life and death, and many Astra Militarum vehicle crews are drilled in these vital skills.

At the start of your turn, roll one D6 for each **VEHICLE** model from your army with this doctrine that has lost any wounds. On a 2-4 that model regains 1 lost wound. On a 5+ that model regains up to D3 lost wounds.

Lords' Approval

Hailing from a world where being seen to fight well in the eyes of one's betters means social advancement, soldiers of this regiment fight hard in the presence of their officers.

When resolving an attack made with a melee weapon by a **<REGIMENT> INFANTRY** model with this doctrine whilst within 9" of a friendly **<REGIMENT> OFFICER** model, improve the Armour Penetration characteristic of that weapon by 1 for that attack (e.g. AP 0 becomes AP -1).

Monster Hunters

The million worlds of the Imperium crawl with myriad deadly xenofauna, and some human populations have become adept at hunting such creatures. When regiments of soldiers are raised from these worlds, their monster-hunting skills prove hugely valuable in battle.

When resolving an attack made with a Heavy weapon by a model with this doctrine against a **MONSTER** unit, an unmodified wound roll of 6 inflicts 1 mortal wound on the target in addition to any other damage.

Slum Fighters

Across the Imperium, billions of its citizens live in untold squalor, in places where might is right and violence is a way of life. Such hardship breeds brutal soldiers who fight as fiercely against the enemies of Mankind as they once did against rival gangs.

When resolving an attack made with a melee weapon by an **INFANTRY** model with this doctrine, an unmodified hit roll of 6 scores 1 additional hit.

'Not many can say they've faced down a Genestealer. Most that have get killed by a different one seconds later. But I can. I've done it more than once. There's something worse about these ones though, the ones that look part-human. They hate you almost as much as you hate them. It's not just animal instinct. You can see it in their eyes, even as they're bleeding out with your bayonet in their throat, their claws still reaching out to slash you up. I pray to the Emperor that I get to kill more. Only extinction's good enough for them.'

- *Veteran Guardsman Garadux,*
Indigan Praefects 47th 'Lictor Killers',
Defence of the Volushun Shipyards

TANK ACES

In the grim dark future of the 41st Millennium, armies of Astra Militarum tanks thousands strong wage war on vast battlefields across countless worlds. Among their number, some commanders and crews become legendary for their skills.

If an **Astra Militarum Character** is your Warlord, rather than determining a Warlord Trait for that model, you can instead select one Tank Ace ability for an **Astra Militarum Vehicle** model from your army. To do so, before the battle begins select one **Astra Militarum Vehicle** model (without the **Brood Brothers** keyword) from your army, and select a Tank Ace ability from the corresponding list below – note that some **Vehicle** models cannot be given Tank Ace abilities. That Tank Ace ability applies to the selected model until the end of the battle. Write down any Tank Ace abilities your models have on your army roster. Named characters cannot be given a Tank Ace ability, and no model can have more than one Tank Ace ability.

If you have an **Astra Militarum Character** model in your army, you also have access to the Tank Ace Stratagem below:

1CP

TANK ACE
Astra Militarum Stratagem
Imperial armoured regiments fight in countless wars across the galaxy. Though many tank crews are lost, some survive a number of battles, their experience and success earning them renown as tank aces.

Use this Stratagem before the battle. Select one **Astra Militarum Vehicle** model (without the **Brood Brothers** keyword) from your army. That model can be given a Tank Ace ability from the corresponding list below. Named characters cannot be given a Tank Ace ability, and no model can have more than one Tank Ace ability. You can only use this Stratagem once per battle.

MAIN BATTLE TANK ACES

If the selected **Vehicle** model has the **Leman Russ** keyword, you can select from the following Tank Ace abilities:

Master Mechanic
The ace knows their vehicle's ways and foibles in great detail, and is able to repair minor damage with ease.

When resolving an attack made with a ranged weapon against this unit, reduce the Damage characteristic of that weapon by 1 (to a minimum of 1) for that attack.

Slow and Purposeful
The ace is incredibly deliberate in their actions, taking their time to make the perfect shot.

In your Shooting phase, when resolving an attack made by this model, if it did not move or moved a distance less than half its Move characteristic in the preceding Movement phase, re-roll a wound roll of 1.

Weapon Expert
The ace has truly mastered their vehicle's primary weapon, using it to deliver killing shots against the odds.

Improve the Armour Penetration characteristic of turret weapons (see *Codex: Astra Militarum*) this model is equipped with by 1 (e.g. AP 0 becomes AP -1).

Armoured Rush
The ace loves nothing more than the thrill of firing their tank's main cannon as they rush at the foe.

In your Shooting phase, this model can shoot with turret weapons it is equipped with even if it Advanced this turn.

Up-armoured
The ace has invested considerable time in bolstering the armour of their vehicle.

This model has a Save characteristic of 2+.

Steel Commander
The ace is a master of conducting armoured warfare, calmly responding to every ebb and flow of battle.

Tank Commander models with this ability can issue one additional Tank Order each turn.

SUPPORT ACES

If the selected **Vehicle** model has the **Basilisk, Wyvern, Hydra, Manticore** or **Deathstrike** keywords, you can select from the following Tank Ace abilities:

Full Payload

The ace always utilises their vehicle's weapons to their fullest effect, determined to destroy their enemies.

Do not roll to determine the Damage characteristic of weapons this model is equipped with; they have their maximum values (e.g. a weapon with a Damage characteristic of D3 inflicts 3 damage).

Shatterer of Will

The ace bombards foes whose morale has been sapped by battle, completely shattering their will to fight on.

In the Shooting phase, after you have resolved all of the attacks made by this model, select one enemy unit that any of those attacks scored a hit against. Until the end of the turn, subtract 2 from the Leadership characteristic of that unit.

Well-stocked Magazines

The ace knows the importance of always having enough ammunition to hand.

When rolling to determine the Type characteristic of a ranged weapon this model is equipped with, you can re-roll any or all of the dice.

SUPER-HEAVY ACES

If the selected **Vehicle** model has the **Titanic** keyword, you can select from the following Tank Ace abilities:

Inspiring Might

Such is the ace's reputation for snatching victory from the jaws of defeat that they are an inspiration to all.

When a Morale test is taken for a friendly **Astra Militarum** unit within 6" of this model, roll one additional D6 and discard one of the dice.

Hull-down Deployment

The tank ace is an expert in maximising the available cover to shield their huge vehicle from attack.

This model receives the benefit of cover until the first time it moves in the battle.

Steadfast Leviathan

This super-heavy tank ace has fought alongside their allies for so long that they have learned to work seamlessly with them and adopt their ways of war.

If your army is Battle-forged, this model gains the Regimental Doctrine of its **<Regiment>** even if it is in a Super-heavy Auxiliary Detachment.

'The Hammerhead's big cannon was pointing straight at us. But then it blew up. "Ironrider" got it in one shot. Must have been her thirty-third kill. Never been so grateful to see that arrogant treadhead.'

- Private Kocha Garrin,
Cadian 1273rd 'Elysion Eagles'
mechanised infantry regiment

ASTRA MILITARUM STRATAGEMS

If your army is Battle-forged and includes any Astra Militarum Detachments (excluding Auxiliary Support Detachments), you have access to the Stratagems shown here, and can spend Command Points to activate them. These reflect the unique strategies used by the forces of the Astra Militarum on the battlefield.

RELENTLESS
Astra Militarum Stratagem

Astra Militarum vehicles are so rugged and robust that they can be pushed beyond their limits temporarily in times of emergency, even if they have sustained damage.

Use this Stratagem at the start of your turn. Select one **Vehicle** model (except a **Titanic** model) that has a damage table on its datasheet. Until the end of that turn, that model uses the top row of its damage table, regardless of how many wounds it has lost.

FURIOUS CHARGE
Astra Militarum Stratagem

The brute power of Ogryns is such that when they charge, the impact is devastating.

Use this Stratagem in your Charge phase, when an **Ogryn** unit from your army finishes a charge move. For each model in that unit, you can select one enemy unit within 1" of that model and roll one D6; on a 4+ that enemy unit suffers 1 mortal wound.

DIRECT ONSLAUGHT
Astra Militarum Stratagem

Normally used for indirect fire missions, when a target becomes visible to Manticores and Wyverns they are capable of unleashing a devastating barrage upon it.

Use this Stratagem in your Shooting phase when a **Manticore** or **Wyvern** model from your army is chosen to shoot with. Until the end of that phase, when resolving an attack made with a storm eagle rocket or wyvern quad stormshard mortar by that model against a unit that is visible to it, add 1 to the hit roll.

SPLASH DAMAGE
Astra Militarum Stratagem

Cover offers little protection against Hellhounds and their variants, and often becomes the target's tomb.

Use this Stratagem in your Shooting phase, when a **Hellhound** model from your army is chosen to shoot with. Until the end of that phase, when resolving an attack made with a chem cannon, inferno cannon or melta cannon by that model against a unit that is receiving the benefit of cover, you can re-roll the wound roll.

EXPERIENCED EYE
Astra Militarum Stratagem

War on numerous battlefields against many foes has taught experienced Astra Militarum soldiers how to identify and exploit weak points in enemy armour.

Use this Stratagem in your Shooting phase, when an **Astra Militarum Veterans** unit from your army is chosen to shoot with. Until the end of that phase, when resolving an attack made with a weapon by a model in that unit, improve the Armour Penetration characteristic of that weapon by 1 for that attack (e.g. AP 0 becomes AP -1).

CONCENTRATED FIRE
Astra Militarum Stratagem

By focusing their fire on one target, gunners can follow their comrades' tracers and maximise damage.

Use this Stratagem in your Shooting phase, when a **Heavy Weapons Squad** unit from your army is chosen to shoot with. Select one enemy unit. Until the end of that phase, attacks made by models in that **Heavy Weapons Squad** unit must target that enemy unit, and when resolving those attacks, add 1 to the hit and wound rolls for any attack made with a weapon from the *Heavy Weapons* list (see *Codex: Astra Militarum*).

STRIKE FIRST, STRIKE HARD
Astra Militarum Stratagem

From advanced positions, Sentinels take careful aim and often strike at key targets before battle begins.

Use this Stratagem in your Shooting phase in the first battle round, when an **ARMOURED SENTINELS** or **SCOUT SENTINELS** unit from your army is chosen to shoot with. Until the end of that phase, when resolving an attack made by a model in that unit, add 2 to the hit roll.

HEAD FIRST
Astra Militarum Stratagem

Mechanised infantry units often drill to strike the enemy hard and fast the instant they disembark.

Use this Stratagem in your Charge phase, when a unit from your army is chosen to charge with. Until the end of that phase, if that unit disembarked from a **CHIMERA** unit this turn, when making a charge roll for that unit, add 2 to the result.

SHIELD OF FLESH
Astra Militarum Stratagem

Heavily armoured and immensely tough, Bullgryns can be a superlative shield against incoming fire.

Use this Stratagem in the Shooting phase, when an **INFANTRY** unit from your army that is within 3" of a friendly **BULLGRYNS** unit is chosen as the target of an attack. Until the end of that phase, when resolving an attack made against that **INFANTRY** unit, if that **BULLGRYNS** unit is closer to the attacking model than that **INFANTRY** unit is, subtract 1 from the hit roll.

FOCUSED BOMBARDMENT
Astra Militarum Stratagem

At the precise moment, the Master of Ordnance calls every gun at their disposal to fire on a single point.

Use this Stratagem in your Shooting phase, when a **MASTER OF ORDNANCE** unit from your army is chosen to shoot with. Until the end of that phase, the artillery barrage that unit is equipped with has a Type characteristic of Heavy 6.

DEFT MANOEUVRING
Astra Militarum Stratagem

When under fire, Armoured Sentinels skilfully manoeuvre to face their front armour towards the enemy.

Use this Stratagem in your opponent's Shooting phase, when an **ARMOURED SENTINELS** unit from your army is chosen as the target for an attack. Until the end of that phase, when resolving an attack made against that unit, halve any damage inflicted (rounding up).

HAIL OF FIRE
Astra Militarum Stratagem

Rapid reloading is at the core of tank crew training.

Use this Stratagem in your Shooting phase, when a **LEMAN RUSS** model from your army is chosen to shoot with. Until the end of that phase, when resolving an attack made with a weapon by that model against a **VEHICLE** unit, do not roll to determine the Type characteristic of that weapon; it has the maximum value (e.g. a Heavy D6 weapon makes 6 shots).

PSYCHIC CONCLAVE
Astra Militarum Stratagem

When they fight together, the psychic power of Primaris Psykers and Wyrdvane Psykers is magnified to a level far greater than the sum of their parts.

Use this Stratagem at the start of your Psychic phase. Select one **WYRDVANE PSYKERS** unit from your army and one friendly **ASTRA MILITARUM PRIMARIS PSYKER** unit within 6" of that **WYRDVANE PSYKERS** unit. Until the end of that phase, when a Psychic test is taken for a model in either of those units, add 2 to the result. In addition, until the end of that phase, each of those units can attempt to manifest one additional psychic power.

ROLLING DEATH
Astra Militarum Stratagem

Taurox drivers strike the perfect balance between advancing and maximising their firepower.

Use this Stratagem in your Shooting phase, when a **TAUROX** model from your army is chosen to shoot with. Until the end of that phase, when resolving an attack made by that model, if that model moved less than half its Move characteristic in the preceding Movement phase, add 1 to the hit roll.

THE ORDO TEMPESTUS

This section contains new and updated rules for the Militarum Tempestus that can be used when fielding a MILITARUM TEMPESTUS Detachment, including Regimental Doctrines, Relics, Warlord Traits and Stratagems.

<TEMPESTUS REGIMENT>

MILITARUM TEMPESTUS units in your army gain the <TEMPESTUS REGIMENT> keyword. When you include a unit with the <TEMPESTUS REGIMENT> keyword in your army, you must nominate which Tempestus Regiment it is from, and then replace all instances of the <TEMPESTUS REGIMENT> keyword on that unit's datasheet with the name of your chosen Tempestus Regiment. The <TEMPESTUS REGIMENT> keyword can only be replaced by one of the following:

- 54TH PSIAN JAKALS
- 32ND THETOID EAGLES
- 133RD LAMBDAN LIONS
- 43RD IOTAN DRAGONS
- 55TH KAPPIC EAGLES
- 9TH IOTAN GORGONNES

If your army contains any units with both the <REGIMENT> and <TEMPESTUS REGIMENT> keywords, you must choose a different keyword to replace each of those keywords on those units' datasheets.

REGIMENTAL DOCTRINES

If your army is Battle-forged, all <TEMPESTUS REGIMENT> units in a MILITARUM TEMPESTUS Detachment gain a Regimental Doctrine selected from those presented on the page opposite, so long as every unit in that Detachment (excluding the Advisors and Auxilla mentioned below) has the same <TEMPESTUS REGIMENT> keyword.

ADVISORS AND AUXILLA

The units listed below can be included in a MILITARUM TEMPESTUS Detachment, despite not having the MILITARUM TEMPESTUS keyword. In addition, they do not prevent other units in that Detachment from gaining a Regimental Doctrine. Note, however, that the units listed below can never themselves benefit from a Regimental Doctrine.

- Tech-Priest Enginseer
- Servitors
- Ministorum Priest
- Crusaders
- AERONAUTICA IMPERIALIS units
- MILITARUM AUXILLA units
- OFFICIO PREFECTUS units
- SCHOLASTICA PSYKANA units

MILITARUM TEMPESTUS REGIMENTAL DOCTRINES

Where the Astra Militarum places importance on huge numbers, the regiments of the Militarum Tempestus emphasise tactical ability, superior weaponry and rigorous training in diverse conditions. As a result, these elite regiments are far more scarce, yet their brave deeds are famed throughout the Imperium.

STORM TROOPERS

The warriors of the Militarum Tempestus are the best of the best, merciless killers trained to obliterate their foes in a pinpoint fusillade of hot-shot las rounds.

See Codex: Astra Militarum.

DEATH FROM THE DARK
54TH PSIAN JAKALS

The Psian Jakals go to war in armour of jet black and with fearsome skulls painted on their masks. This, combined with incredible tracking skills and determination, makes them a truly terrifying enemy.

Each model destroyed by an attack made by a model with this doctrine in your Shooting phase is treated as 2 destroyed models in the following Morale phase.

PREDATORY STRIKE
32ND THETOID EAGLES

Known for their particularly vicious methods of warfare, the 32nd Thetoid Eagles are specialists in close-ranged firefights and rarely take prisoners.

When resolving an attack made with a ranged weapon by a model with this doctrine against a unit that is within half range, an unmodified hit roll of 6 scores 1 additional hit.

PRIZED WEAPONRY
133RD LAMBDAN LIONS

The 133rd Lambdan Lions work extensively with the Adeptus Mechanicus in the recovery of lost knowledge and arcane technologies. In exchange for their service, the Adeptus Mechanicus sees fit to reward them with esoteric augmentations for their vehicles, armour and weaponry.

Improve the Armour Penetration characteristic of weapons models with this doctrine are equipped with by 1 (e.g. AP 0 becomes AP -1).

CRACK SHOTS
43RD IOTAN DRAGONS

Highly adept in counter-insurgency operations, the 43rd Iotan Dragons learn their patient and bloody trade in darkened cave labyrinths. Experts in combatting Tyranid Genestealers and other outlier organisms, they have learned the importance of being able to fire with precision rapidly even at longer ranges. Those who cannot do this are slaughtered by their preternaturally fast enemies.

Add 6" to the Range characteristic of Rapid Fire weapons models with this doctrine are equipped with.

MOBILISED INFANTRY
55TH KAPPIC EAGLES

A regiment with a long and illustrious history of defeating the Emperor's foes, the 55th Kappic Eagles typify the obedience, excellence and efficiency for which the Militarum Tempestus is renowned.

INFANTRY models with this doctrine do not suffer the penalty for moving and firing Heavy weapons. When resolving an attack made by a model with this doctrine in a turn in which it disembarked from a **TRANSPORT**, add 1 to the hit roll.

RESOLUTE HEROISM
9TH IOTAN GORGONNES

The 9th Iotan Gorgonnes frequently fight alongside the Adepta Sororitas Order of the Glowing Chalice, both forces having originated from the same Schola Progenium facility of Vedill I. Their allies' devotion to the Imperial Creed inspires them to seek the utter destruction of their enemies.

When resolving an attack made with a ranged weapon by an **INFANTRY** model with this doctrine against the closest enemy unit, an unmodified hit roll of 6 scores 1 additional hit.

HEIRLOOMS OF THE REGIMENTS

If your army is led by a Warlord in a **MILITARUM TEMPESTUS** Detachment, you can give one of the following Relics to a **CHARACTER** model in a **MILITARUM TEMPESTUS** Detachment from your army instead of giving them a Relic from *Codex: Astra Militarum*.

Note that some Relics are weapons that replace one of the model's existing weapons. Where this is the case, you must, if you are using points values, still pay the cost of the weapon that is being replaced. Write down any Relics your models have on your army roster.

THE HOUND'S TEETH

The machine spirit of this ferocious weapon has a deep hatred for the Aeldari, against whom the 54th Psian Jakals have fought bitter guerilla wars for years.

54TH PSIAN JAKALS model equipped with a chainsword only. This Relic replaces a chainsword and has the following profile:

WEAPON	RANGE	TYPE	S	AP	D
The Hound's Teeth	Melee	Melee	+1	-2	2
Abilities: When the bearer fights, it makes 3 additional attacks with this weapon. When resolving an attack made with this weapon against an **AELDARI** unit, you can re-roll the wound roll.					

FIRE OF JUDGEMENT

This weapon slew countless cultists during the Xinon Wars, honouring the vicious Scions it belongs to.

32ND THETOID EAGLES model equipped with a hot-shot laspistol only. This Relic replaces a hot-shot laspistol and has the following profile:

WEAPON	RANGE	TYPE	S	AP	D
Fire of Judgement	12"	Pistol 2	3	*	*
Abilities: When resolving an attack made with this weapon, a successful hit roll inflicts 1 mortal wound on the target and the attack sequence ends.					

REFRACTOR FIELD GENERATOR

The Adeptus Mechanicus gifted the 133rd Lambdan Lions with this advanced refractor field generator after the Lions successfully cleansed Lurea IX of a Genestealer infestation.

133RD LAMBDAN LIONS model only. Friendly **133RD LAMBDAN LIONS** models have a 5+ invulnerable save whilst within 6" of a model from your army with this Relic.

EMPEROR'S FURY

The wielder of this weapon brings the fury of a sun into every subterranean hellhole.

43RD IOTAN DRAGONS model equipped with a plasma pistol only. This Relic replaces a plasma pistol and has the following profile:

WEAPON	RANGE	TYPE	S	AP	D
Emperor's Fury When you choose this weapon to shoot with, select one of the profiles below.					
- Standard	12"	Pistol 3	7	-3	1
- Supercharge	12"	Pistol 3	8	-3	2
Abilities: If any hit rolls of 1 are made for attacks with this weapon's supercharge profile, the bearer is destroyed after shooting with this weapon.					

DISTRACTION CHARGES

The 55th Kappic Eagles deploy these charges, packed with stunshot and smoke canisters, to disrupt attacking troops while the Scions manoeuvre to another position.

55TH KAPPIC EAGLES model only. When resolving an Overwatch attack made by a friendly **55TH KAPPIC EAGLES** model within 3" of a model with this Relic, if that attack scores a hit, the target is slowed until the end of the phase. When a charge roll is made for a slowed unit, halve the result (rounding up).

BLESSED BOLTGUN

Two-dozen sisters of the Order of the Glowing Chalice have prayed over this holy boltgun.

9TH IOTAN GORGONNES model equipped with a boltgun only. This Relic replaces a boltgun and has the following profile:

WEAPON	RANGE	TYPE	S	AP	D
Blessed boltgun	12"	Rapid Fire 1	5	-2	2
Abilities: This weapon can target a **CHARACTER** unit even if it is not the closest enemy unit. When resolving an attack made with this weapon against a **PSYKER** unit, this weapon has a Damage characteristic of 3 for that attack.					

MILITARUM TEMPESTUS WARLORD TRAITS

The troops of the Militarum Tempestus are bred for war. They are unshakeable in their faith and possessed of immense surety of purpose. Their Tempestor Primes are highly experienced soldiers, who in their long careers develop unique skills, characters and tastes in battle.

If a **MILITARUM TEMPESTUS** unit in a **MILITARUM TEMPESTUS** Detachment from your army is your Warlord, you can pick a Militarum Tempestus Warlord Trait from the list below instead of from the Warlord Traits table in *Codex: Astra Militarum*, but only if your Warlord is from the relevant Tempestus Regiment.

SKILLED TRACKER
54TH PSIAN JAKALS

The warlord has developed his proficiency in hunting and surveillance to levels bordering on prescience, and always knows where best to deploy his warriors.

At the start of the first battle round, before the first turn begins, select up to three **54TH PSIAN JAKALS** units from your army on the battlefield. Remove those units from the battlefield then set them up again as described in the Deployment section of the mission being played (if both players have abilities that redeploy units, roll off; the winner chooses who redeploys their units first).

UNCOMPROMISING PROSECUTION
32ND THETOID EAGLES

The warlord has taught his troops to always aim for a target's most vulnerable points, to maximise the damage they suffer in combat.

When resolving an attack made with a hot-shot lasgun, hot-shot laspistol or hot-shot volley gun by a friendly **32ND THETOID EAGLES** model whilst within 6" of this Warlord, on an unmodified wound roll of 6 that weapon has an Armour Penetration characteristic of -4 for that attack.

KEYS TO THE ARMOURY
133RD LAMBDAN LIONS

The warlord has access to rare equipment, such as unusual augur arrays and oculus equipment normally kept by the Adeptus Mechanicus for its own use.

Re-roll hit rolls of 1 for attacks made with ranged weapons by models in friendly **133RD LAMBDAN LIONS** units whilst their unit is within 6" of this Warlord.

PRECISION TARGETING
43RD IOTAN DRAGONS

The warlord is a mathematical genius as well as a highly experienced combatant. Combined, these skills make him extremely adept at pinpointing where an enemy will be and directing accurate and lethal fire against them.

At the start of your Shooting phase, select one enemy unit within 18" of this Warlord. Until the end of that phase, when resolving an attack made by a friendly **43RD IOTAN DRAGONS** model whilst its unit is within 6" of this Warlord, that enemy unit does not receive the benefit of cover.

MASTER VOX
55TH KAPPIC EAGLES

The warlord has in his possession a master vox with which he can directly command his forces over a wide area, enacting far-ranging strategies.

When using this Warlord's Voice of Command ability, it can issue orders to friendly **55TH KAPPIC EAGLES INFANTRY** units within 24". In addition, while this Warlord is embarked within a **TRANSPORT** model it can still use its Voice of Command ability; when doing so, make any measurements from that **TRANSPORT** model's hull.

SANCTITY OF SPIRIT
9TH IOTAN GORGONNES

The warlord has fought on multiple battlefields with his regiment's allies of the Order of the Glowing Chalice. They have been blessed countless times by the battle sisters, and have drunk sacred water from holy cups held by the Order's preceptories. As a result the warlord's roll of honour from fighting for the Ecclesiarchy is as long as he is tall, extolling him as a beacon of faith.

When a Psychic test is taken for an enemy **PSYKER** model within 24" of this Warlord, that model suffers Perils of the Warp on a roll of any double.

MILITARUM TEMPESTUS STRATAGEMS

If your army is Battle-forged and includes any Militarum Tempestus Detachments (excluding Auxiliary Support Detachments), you have access to the Stratagems shown here, and can spend Command Points to activate them. When one of these Stratagems refers to a unit from your army, that unit must be in a Militarum Tempestus Detachment from your army.

POINT-BLANK EFFICACY

1CP

Militarum Tempestus Stratagem

When timed correctly, a hail of hot-shot las at close range can be devastating to the enemy.

Use this Stratagem in your Shooting phase, when a **MILITARUM TEMPESTUS** unit from your army is chosen to shoot with. Until the end of that phase, when resolving an attack made with a hot-shot lasgun, hot-shot laspistol or hot-shot volley gun by a model in that unit against a unit within half range, add 1 to the Strength characteristic of that weapon for that attack.

HAMMER BLOW

2CP

Militarum Tempestus Stratagem

The concentrated firepower of Imperial aircraft is so overwhelming that it can pin down the enemy and deny them whole areas of the battlefield.

Use this Stratagem in your Shooting phase, when a model is destroyed by an attack made by an **AERONAUTICA IMPERIALIS** model with the Flyer Battlefield Role from your army. That destroyed model's unit is pinned until the start of your next turn. Halve the result of any Advance and charge rolls made for pinned units. When resolving an attack made with a ranged weapon by a model from a pinned unit, subtract 1 from the hit roll.

UNQUESTIONING OBEDIENCE

1CP

Militarum Tempestus Stratagem

The soldiers of the Militarum Tempestus are renowned for their staunch discipline and unwavering obedience.

Use this Stratagem in the Morale phase. Select one **TEMPESTOR PRIME** or **COMMISSAR** model from your army. Until the end of that phase, when a Morale test is taken for a friendly **MILITARUM TEMPESTUS** unit within 12" of that model, do not roll the dice; it is automatically passed.

ADVANCED COUNTER-MEASURES

1CP

Militarum Tempestus Stratagem

When expecting to insert into particularly perilous drop zones, Tempestus Scions fit their dropships with additional defences to ward off incoming fire.

Use this Stratagem before the battle. Select one **VALKYRIE** model from your army. When you declare that model will hover, it does not lose the Hard to Hit ability.

PRECISION DROP

1CP

Militarum Tempestus Stratagem

So skilled are some Tempestus Scions at combat drops that they can undertake aerial insertions that would be simply impossible for other troops.

Use this Stratagem in your Movement phase. Select one **AERONAUTICA IMPERIALIS** model with the Flyer Battlefield Role and the Grav-chute Insertion ability from your army. Until the end of that phase, when a **MILITARUM TEMPESTUS** unit with the Aerial Drop ability embarked aboard that model disembarks, that unit must be set up more than 5" away from any enemy models, instead of more than 9". In addition, if that model moved more than 20" that phase, do not roll a D6 for each model disembarking; no models are destroyed.

TACTICAL AIR CONTROL

1CP

Militarum Tempestus Stratagem

Many Tempestus Scions receive advanced training in calling for devastating air strikes and strafing runs.

Use this Stratagem at the start of your Shooting phase. Select one **OFFICER OF THE FLEET** model from your army. Until the end of that phase, when picking an enemy unit for that model's Air Raid Requested or Strafing Coordinates abilities, you can measure the range and visibility from any friendly **MILITARUM TEMPESTUS** unit on the battlefield that has a vox-caster, instead of from that model. When rolling a D6 for that model's Air Raid Requested ability, add 2 to the roll.

PROGENY OF CONFLICT

1CP

Militarum Tempestus Stratagem

The Scions are bred for war, each a born leader.

Use this Stratagem before the battle, after nominating your Warlord. Select one **Militarum Tempestus Character** model from your army that does not have a Warlord Trait and determine one Warlord Trait for it; it is regarded as your Warlord for the purposes of that Warlord Trait. Each Warlord Trait in your army must be unique (if randomly generated, re-roll duplicate results). You can only use this Stratagem once per battle.

KILLING ZONE

1CP

Militarum Tempestus Stratagem

Tempestus Scions frequently use fields of enfilading fire to destroy their enemies.

Use this Stratagem in your Shooting phase, after you have shot with a **<Tempestus Regiment> Infantry** unit from your army. Select one enemy unit that had any models destroyed as a result of attacks made by models from that unit in that phase. Until the end of that phase, when resolving an attack made by a friendly **<Tempestus Regiment> Infantry** model against that enemy unit, add 1 to the wound roll.

TACTICAL MISDIRECTION

1CP

55th Kappic Eagles Stratagem

The 55th Kappic Eagles destroy each target for a reason.

Use this Stratagem in your Shooting phase, when a unit is destroyed by an attack made by a model in a **55th Kappic Eagles** unit from your army. In your opponent's next Shooting phase, when resolving an attack made by an enemy model against a unit other than that **55th Kappic Eagles** unit, subtract 1 from the hit roll if that **55th Kappic Eagles** unit is the closest visible unit from your army to that model.

DRILLED TO PERFECTION

1CP

43rd Iotan Dragons Stratagem

The 43rd stand firm, weapons readied, before their foe.

Use this Stratagem in your opponent's Charge phase, before a **43rd Iotan Dragons** unit from your army fires Overwatch. Until the end of that phase, when resolving an Overwatch attack made by a model in that unit, a hit roll of 4+ scores a hit.

ELUSIVE HUNTERS

1CP

54th Psian Jakals Stratagem

The 54th Psian Jakals are masters of camouflage.

Use this Stratagem in your opponent's Shooting phase, when a **54th Psian Jakals** unit from your army is chosen as the target of an attack. Until the end of that phase, when resolving an attack made with a ranged weapon by an enemy model against that unit whilst that unit is not within half range, subtract 1 from the hit roll.

GIFTS FROM THE MECHANICUS

1CP

133rd Lambdan Lions Stratagem

Many squads of the 133rd Lambdan Lions have been gifted with enhanced power packs for their weapons.

Use this Stratagem in your Shooting phase, when a **133rd Lambdan Lions** unit from your army is chosen to shoot with. Until the end of that phase, when resolving an attack made with a hot-shot lasgun, hot-shot laspistol or hot-shot volley gun by a model in that unit, an unmodified wound roll of 6 inflicts 1 mortal wound on the target and the attack sequence ends.

FULL CHARGE

1CP

32nd Thetoid Eagles Stratagem

Mounted in rapid Taurox Primes, the 32nd Thetoid Eagles unleash hell upon the enemy at close range.

Use this Stratagem in your Shooting phase, when a **32nd Thetoid Eagles Taurox Prime** model from your army is chosen to shoot with. Until the end of that phase, when resolving an attack made by that model against an enemy unit within 12", you can re-roll the hit roll.

DARING DESCENT

1CP

9th Iotan Gorgonnes Stratagem

Incredibly courageous, the 9th drop into the hotzone.

Use this Stratagem in your Movement phase. Select one **9th Iotan Gorgonnes** unit from your army that was set up in a high-altitude transport. Until the end of that phase, when you set up that unit on the battlefield using the Aerial Drop ability, that unit must be set up more than 5" away from any enemy models, instead of more than 9". You cannot charge with that unit this turn.

GENESTEALER CULTS

THE LURKERS BENEATH

This section contains new and updated rules for *Codex: Genestealer Cults*, including Stratagems, psychic powers, rules for creating custom Cult Creeds and the latest errata updates. This section also includes a name generator.

Errata

Presented below and opposite are some of the rules from *Codex: Genestealer Cults* with errata updates included.

Cult Creeds

Pages 74-75 present rules for creating your own Cult Creeds. These comprise a selection of abilities that can be combined instead of choosing a Cult Creed from *Codex: Genestealer Cults*.

Stratagems

Pages 76-77 present new Stratagems that can be used by **Genestealer Cults** Detachments in addition to those found in *Codex: Genestealer Cults*, bringing new tactical options and unique behaviours to the minions of the Patriarch.

Cult Psychic Powers

On page 78 you will find new cult-specific psychic powers, allowing the unique psychic footprints of certain cults to manifest themselves on the battlefield in new and dangerous ways.

Name Generator

Page 79 presents a D66 table packed with thematic names for your Genestealer Cultists. You can use this to randomly generate or pick names for your warriors, or simply as a source of inspiration for inventing names of your own.

'Patients 1-11, dead. Patients 12-57, dying. Patients 58-234, viable. Patients 235-422, ready. After seven months, the serum is finished. Inform the Primus. Ask him for two thousand more subjects. Once they are complete, then he will have his war.'

- Pike Garleon, Biophagus

ERRATA

Presented here are two rules from *Codex: Genestealer Cults* reprinted to include the latest updates and errata.

Cult Ambush

Genestealer Cults plan meticulously before rising up against their oppressors, remaining hidden until the moment of ascension arrives.

During deployment, you can set up this unit in ambush instead of on the battlefield. If this unit has the **Infantry** or **Biker** keyword, you can either set it up in ambush or underground instead of on the battlefield.

When you set up a unit underground, it can emerge at the end of any of your Movement phases – set the unit up anywhere on the battlefield that is more than 9" from any enemy models.

When you set up a unit in ambush, place one ambush marker anywhere on the battlefield that is wholly within your deployment zone. You will need one ambush marker for each unit that will deploy in this way. If you set up a **Transport** model in ambush, you must still tell your opponent what units are embarked within it when it is set up in ambush – do not set up separate ambush markers for units that start the battle embarked within a **Transport** model, even if they have the Cult Ambush ability.

Ambush markers are not units and cannot be targeted, attacked or destroyed. When measuring to or from ambush markers, always measure to the centre of the marker. If you are playing a mission that uses Concealed Deployment, the Concealed Deployment rules only apply to units that do not have the Cult Ambush ability. If you are playing a mission that uses Sentries, Sentry models cannot be set up in ambush, even if they have the Cult Ambush ability.

Matched Play: In matched play, units set up in ambush using this rule count as being set up on the battlefield for the purposes of Tactical Reserves.

Revealing Ambush Markers

If you have the first turn, you must reveal all of your ambush markers at the start of your Movement phase, one at a time, before moving any units. Each time you reveal an ambush marker, select one unit from your army that you set up in ambush, then set up one model from that unit within 1" of that ambush marker. Then remove that marker before setting up the rest of that model's unit wholly within 6" of the first model, wholly within your deployment zone and more than 9" from any enemy models (any models that cannot be placed are destroyed). If it is your turn, that unit can still move and shoot normally during the turn it is set up, but if it is a **Transport**, units that disembark from it this turn cannot be set up within 9" of any enemy models. Note that unless these units actually move during this Movement phase, they do not count as having moved in their Movement phase for any rules purposes, such as shooting Heavy weapons.

If your opponent has the first turn, then none of their units can be set up or end a move within 9" of any of your ambush markers. At the end of your opponent's first Movement phase, after they have set up all of their units from reinforcements (if any), reveal all of your ambush markers as described above before continuing with the turn.

Brood Brothers

Several **Genestealer Cults** units also have the **Brood Brothers** keyword. These units can be included in a **Genestealer Cults** Detachment without preventing other units in that Detachment from gaining a Cult Creed. Note, however, that **Brood Brothers** units do not themselves benefit from any Cult Creed.

In addition, to represent Astra Militarum forces that have been subverted, you can include **Astra Militarum** units and **Genestealer Cults** units in the same matched play army, even though these units do not have any Faction keywords in common. In such cases, ignore the **Astra Militarum** units when choosing your army's Faction.

If your army is Battle-forged, you can only include one **Astra Militarum** Detachment (one in which every unit has the **Astra Militarum** keyword) in your army for each **Genestealer Cults** Detachment in that army. You cannot include **Astra Militarum** named characters in these Detachments, and these Detachments cannot be Specialist Detachments. These **Astra Militarum** Detachments are then known as **Brood Brothers** Detachments, and every unit in them that has the <**Regiment**> or **Militarum Tempestus** keyword must replace it in every instance on its datasheet with **Brood Brothers** (if a unit does not have either of these keywords, it simply gains the **Brood Brothers** keyword).

Brood Brothers Detachments do not gain any of the Detachment abilities listed in *Codex: Astra Militarum*, such as Regimental Doctrines, nor can they use any regiment-specific Stratagems, Orders etc. Furthermore, **Infantry** models in **Brood Brothers** Detachments increase their Leadership characteristic by 1 and they gain the Unquestioning Loyalty ability (see *Codex: Genestealer Cults*). Units in **Brood Brothers** Detachments do not gain the Cult Ambush ability. Your Warlord cannot be from a **Brood Brothers** Detachment, and you cannot give any Relics to **Brood Brothers Characters**. In addition, the Command Benefits of all **Brood Brothers** Detachments included in your army in this way are halved (rounding up). This reflects that such Detachments are not a Genestealer Cult's primary fighting force, and the acquisition of such military assets is costly in terms of resource. The Command Benefits of Auxiliary Support Detachments are unaffected.

Orders

Brood Brothers units that have the Voice of Command or Tank Orders abilities (see *Codex: Astra Militarum*) cannot issue orders to any unit that has the **Genestealer Cults** Faction keyword, nor can they issue orders to units that they would not have been able to issue orders to before they gained the **Brood Brothers** keyword (e.g. a **Brood Brothers Company Commander** cannot issue orders to a **Brood Brothers Ogryn** unit or to a **Brood Brothers Tempestus Scions** unit).

Transports

Brood Brothers Taurox Primes can only transport 10 **Brood Brothers Officio Prefectus Infantry** models or 10 **Infantry** models that replaced their **Militarum Tempestus** keyword with **Brood Brothers**.

CULT CREEDS

Each Genestealer Cult has its own dogma, subcultures and battle doctrines. In some cults these variations are subtle, while others are gulfs apart in their preferred means of uprising. Whatever the case, all fight tirelessly until their day of ascendance arrives, and they are united with the Star Children at last.

Codex: Genestealer Cults describes how the <**Cult**> keyword can be substituted with the name of your chosen cult, as well as describing the abilities that units in **Genestealer Cults** Detachments gain. One of these abilities is Cult Creeds. If your chosen cult does not have an associated Cult Creed in *Codex: Genestealer Cults*, you can create its Cult Creed by selecting two rules from the following list:

Hunter's Instincts

Though the Genestealer infection changes all those it touches into fierce predators, in some the hunting instincts are even stronger. These creatures will stop at nothing to find and butcher their prey.

Until the end of the first battle round, add 1 to Advance and charge rolls made for units with this Cult Creed.

Innate Fighters

The bowels of worlds all over the Imperium are home to scum that spend every waking moment either fighting or thinking about the next fight. Once these violent beings are infected by the Genestealer Curse, they become deadlier fighters still.

When resolving an attack made with a melee weapon by a model with this Cult Creed in a turn in which it made a charge move, was charged or performed a Heroic Intervention, re-roll a hit roll of 1.

Thralls of the Patriarch

The Genestealer Cultists of this creed are so enamoured by the power and influence of their Patriarch that there are few things they will not do, few risks they will not take, for their liege's approval.

When a Morale test is taken for a unit with this Cult Creed, halve the number of models that flee (rounding up).

Seasoned Enforcers

There is no true limit on a world to where the claws of the cult cannot reach. Enforcers, those who job it is to quell infestation and rebellion, are as vulnerable as any others to infiltration. Their access to heavy military gear, as well as the training to use it, makes them invaluable.

Infantry models with this Cult Creed do not suffer the penalty for moving and firing Heavy weapons.

Agile Outriders

On worlds defined by vast toxic wastes and rad-choked deserts, the people learn how to traverse the dangerous lands at speed and defend themselves on the move. Genestealer Cults that infect such populations are naturally drawn to mobile warfare.

Biker models with this Cult Creed do not suffer the penalty for moving and firing Heavy weapons and do not suffer the penalty for Advancing and firing Assault weapons.

Armour-piercing Ammunition

Many creeds expend a great deal of effort securing military-grade weapons and armaments in readiness for the inevitable uprising. Some are so successful that they acquire wargear of especially high quality, including specialist ammunition.

When resolving an attack made with an autopistol, autogun or heavy stubber by a model with this Cult Creed against a unit that is within half range, that weapon has an Armour Penetration characteristic of -1 for that attack.

Munitions Experts

The cultists of this creed once worked in munitions plants, producing armaments and explosives for the Imperial war effort – skills they now offer to the Star Children.

Add 1 to the Strength characteristic of Grenade weapons models with this Cult Creed are equipped with.

Unnatural Symbiosis

Tapping into their deep psychic link with the Acolytes and hybrids of their cult, psykers following this creed are able to greatly enhance their powers.

When a Psychic test is taken for a <**Cult**> model with this Cult Creed within 6" of another friendly <**Cult**> unit, you can re-roll any or all dice rolls of 1.

Workers Arisen

The peoples of Imperial worlds throughout the galaxy are worked to the bone in factories, mines and quarries. They slave away for a cause that is never explained, toiling for absent masters. When hope is offered, when they hear that the true Emperor wants to liberate them, they rise up and turn their heavy industrial tools upon their oppressors.

When resolving an attack made with a weapon from the *Heavy Mining Weapons* list (see *Codex: Genestealer Cults*) by a model with this Cult Creed, you can re-roll the hit roll.

Devout Worshippers

The Cult has been blessed with countless Hybrid Metamorphs, and its members know that soon the Star Children will be with them. As such they fight all the harder, rushing into the fray to impress the blessed ones and earn special regard from their approaching deities.

When a charge roll is made for a <CULT> unit with this Cult Creed whilst within 3" of a friendly <CULT> HYBRID METAMORPHS unit, you can re-roll the dice. This Cult Creed cannot be selected together with the Hunter's Instincts Cult Creed.

Poisoned Blades

Whilst savage claws and wicked blades are potent weapons in their own right, some cults go further, lacing them with foul toxins derived from local pollutants or synthesised in laboratories hidden far from sight.

When resolving an attack made with a bonesword, a lash whip and bonesword, or a cultist knife by a model with this Cult Creed, on an unmodified hit roll of 6 you can make one additional attack against the same unit using the same weapon. This additional attack cannot generate another attack.

'Denying the enemy military assets is one thing. Bringing them over to our cause is another. It should always be a priority. To do otherwise would be to waste our gods-given intellect.'

- Nexos Gurnst Vedulschein

GENESTEALER CULTS STRATAGEMS

If your army is Battle-forged and includes any GENESTEALER CULTS Detachments (excluding Auxiliary Support Detachments), you have access to the Stratagems shown here, and can spend Command Points to activate them. These reflect the unique strategies used by the forces of the Genestealer Cults on the battlefield.

PREPARED AMBUSH
1CP

Genestealer Cults Stratagem

Neophyte Hybrids often wait in ambush for many hours, fully prepared for the perfect moment to strike.

Use this Stratagem at the start of your Shooting phase. Select one NEOPHYTE HYBRIDS unit from your army that was set up on the battlefield using the Cult Ambush ability in this battle round. Until the end of that phase, autoguns models in that unit are equipped with have a Type characteristic of Assault 2.

CLOSE-RANGE SHOOT-OUT
1CP

Genestealer Cults Stratagem

Atalan Jackals are experts in hit-and-run attacks and close-range firefights. Combined, these skills are deadly.

Use this Stratagem in your Shooting phase, when an ATALAN JACKALS unit from your army is chosen to shoot with. Until the end of that phase, when resolving an attack made with a Pistol or Assault weapon by a model in that unit against an enemy unit within 12", you can re-roll the wound roll.

ANNIHILATING ADVANCE
1CP

Genestealer Cults Stratagem

Standing in the path of an advancing Goliath Rockgrinder is an act of suicide.

Use this Stratagem in your Charge phase, when a GOLIATH ROCKGRINDER unit from your army finishes a charge move. Select one enemy INFANTRY unit within 1" of that unit, and roll one D6; on a 2+ that enemy unit suffers D3 mortal wounds.

VIOLENCE UNLEASHED
1CP

Genestealer Cults Stratagem

Hybrid Metamorphs resort to an uncontrolled, bestial savagery to slay their foe at close quarters.

Use this Stratagem in the Fight phase, when a HYBRID METAMORPHS unit from your army is chosen to fight with. Until the end of that phase, add 1 to the Attacks characteristic of models in that unit.

INTEGRATED VOX-NET
2CP

Genestealer Cults Stratagem

When equipped with an integrated vox-net, the Jackal Alphus can mark targets for their gene-sect with ease.

Use this Stratagem at the start of your Shooting phase. Select one JACKAL ALPHUS model from your army. Until the end of that phase, replace that model's Priority Target Sighted ability with the following:

'Vox Contact: At the start of your Shooting phase, select one enemy unit within 36" and visible to this model. Until the end of that phase, when resolving an attack made by a friendly <CULT> model against that unit whilst that model is within 18" of this model, add 1 to the hit roll. An enemy unit can only be selected as the target of this ability or the Priority Target Sighted ability once per phase.'

COMMANDING AMPLIFICATION
1CP

Genestealer Cults Stratagem

The Clamavus throws every ounce of their strength into the most rousing speech of their lives.

Use this Stratagem before the battle. Select one CLAMAVUS model from your army. The range of that model's Proclamator Hailer ability is increased by 3". The same model cannot be selected by this Stratagem more than once per battle.

THE GNARLED FIST
1CP

Genestealer Cults Stratagem

Some Abominants are blessed by the Star Children more than others, and these the Aberrants follow adoringly.

Use this Stratagem before the battle. Select one ABOMINANT unit from your army. That unit's The Chosen One ability affects friendly <CULT> ABERRANT units within 9" of that unit, instead of within 6". You can only use this Stratagem once per battle.

RAKING FIRE
1CP

Genestealer Cults Stratagem

At great speed, Achilles Ridgerunners roar into optimal firing positions to inflict catastrophic damage.

Use this Stratagem in your Shooting phase. Select one **Achilles Ridgerunners** unit from your army. Until the end of the turn, when resolving an attack made with a heavy stubber by a model in that unit, add 1 to the hit and wound rolls.

THE CULT'S PSYCHE
1CP

Genestealer Cults Stratagem

Maguses descended from the same line often have enormously strong psychic bonds.

Use this Stratagem before the battle. Select one **<Cult> Magus** unit from your army. That unit can attempt to manifest one additional psychic power in your Psychic phase. When a Psychic test is taken for that unit, add 1 to the total for each other friendly **<Cult> Psyker** unit within 3" (to a maximum of +3). You can only use this Stratagem once per battle.

SLIPPING THROUGH THE SHADOWS
1CP

Genestealer Cults Stratagem

Finding impossible pathways through the battlefield, the Sanctus makes straight for its doomed quarry.

Use this Stratagem in your Movement phase, when a **Sanctus** unit is chosen to move. Until the end of that phase, when that unit Advances, add 6" to its Move characteristic until the end of that phase instead of making an Advance roll. In addition, until the end of the turn, that unit can be chosen to charge with even if they Advanced this turn.

GENETIC LINEAGE
1CP

Genestealer Cults Stratagem

So strong is the Genestealer influence on the psyches of Acolyte Hybrids that occasionally their bestial nature takes over. The consequences are always bloody.

Use this Stratagem in the Charge phase. Select one **Acolyte Hybrids** unit from your army. Until the end of that phase, that unit can be chosen to charge with even if it Advanced this turn.

EVASIVE DRIVING
1CP

Genestealer Cults Stratagem

Many Genestealer Cultists have spent years driving Goliaths. In battle they put this experience to great use.

Use this Stratagem in your opponent's Shooting phase, when a **Goliath Rockgrinder** or **Goliath Truck** unit from your army is chosen as the target of an attack made with a ranged weapon. Until the end of that phase, weapons with an Armour Penetration characteristic of -1 or -2 are treated as having an Armour Penetration characteristic of 0 when resolving an attack against that unit.

OVERCHARGED WEAPONRY
1CP

Genestealer Cults Stratagem

Some cultists take immense pleasure in supercharging their heavy weaponry to butcher their oppressors.

Use this Stratagem in your Shooting phase, when a **<Cult>** unit from your army is chosen to shoot with. Until the end of that phase, when resolving an attack made with a clearance incinerator, heavy mining laser or heavy seismic cannon by a model in that unit, add 1 to the wound roll.

THE HEART OF THE CREED
1CP

Genestealer Cults Stratagem

Some Primuses are devious planners even beyond what is normal for their ilk.

Use this Stratagem before the battle. Select one **<Cult> Primus** model from your army. When that model is set up on the battlefield for the first time, you can select one additional enemy unit for that model's Meticulous Planner ability. You can only use this Stratagem once per battle.

CULT PSYCHIC POWERS

Though the Patriarchs and Maguses of the Genestealer Cults share many psychic gifts, each cult also develops distinctive psychic abilities, shaped by their own beliefs and subcultures and the unique environments in which they arose.

All <Cult> Psyker models can know the psychic power of their respective cult. Instead of generating a psychic power from the Broodmind discipline (see *Codex: Genestealer Cults*), a <Cult> Psyker can instead know the appropriate Cult psychic power from the list below.

CULT OF THE FOUR-ARMED EMPEROR: UNDERMINE

With arms raised, the psyker closes their eyes and pictures the ground beneath the enemy opening up like the maw of a hungry beast. The psyker's eyes open; the enemy is gone, consumed by the rocks and the earth just as they had willed it.

Undermine has a warp charge value of 8. If manifested, select one enemy **Infantry** unit within 18" of this psyker. Until the start of your next Psychic phase, halve the Movement characteristic of models in that unit and halve any Advance or charge rolls made for that unit (rounding up).

THE HIVECULT: SYNAPTIC BLAST

When the forces of the Hivecult fight, their residual psychic energy is palpable to their psykers, who allow its immense power to flow through them before unleashing it upon the enemy in a devastating blast.

Synaptic Blast has a warp charge value of 6. If manifested, select one enemy unit within 18" of and visible to this psyker. Roll a number of D6 equal to the number of **Hivecult** models from your army within 3" of that unit; for each roll of 6 that unit suffers 1 mortal wound.

THE BLADED COG: UNDYING VIGOUR

The psyker harnesses the bio-electricity in the cyborg cultists around them, strengthening their already enhanced physical forms to make them even more resistant to enemy attacks.

Undying Vigour has a warp charge value of 6. If manifested, select one **Bladed Cog** unit from your army within 12" of this psyker. Until the start of your next Psychic phase, when a model in that unit would lose a wound, roll one D6; on a 5+ that wound is not lost.

THE RUSTED CLAW: INESCAPABLE DECAY

With but a glance and a hand gesture from a Rusted Claw psyker, enemy vehicles enter rapid-onset decay. Iron rusts, copper is stained with verdigris and oils dry. Vehicles weakened in such a way are then set upon and ripped apart by the psyker's cultist brethren.

Inescapable Decay has a warp charge value of 6. If manifested, select one enemy **Vehicle** unit within 18" of and visible to this psyker. Until the end of the turn, when resolving an attack made with a weapon against that unit, improve the Armour Penetration characteristic of that weapon by 1 for that attack (e.g. AP 0 becomes AP -1).

THE PAUPER PRINCES: LAST GASP

Even as Pauper Princes cultists fall, their psykers reach out to the last vestiges of life in their broken bodies, gifting them with energy enough for one last hate-filled shot or vicious claw swipe before they finally expire.

Last Gasp has a warp charge value of 7. If manifested, select one **Pauper Princes** unit from your army within 12" of this psyker. Until the start of your next Psychic phase, when a model in that unit is destroyed, roll one D6 before removing that model from play. On a 4+ that model can either shoot with one of its ranged weapons as if it were your Shooting phase, or make one attack with one of its melee weapons as if it were the Fight phase.

THE TWISTED HELIX: MUTAGENIC DEVIATION

Such is a Twisted Helix psyker's genetic connection with the faithful throng fighting around them that they can manipulate the very gene-coding that holds their brethren's bodies together, creating hideous and lethal deviations that assault the enemy with overwhelming ferocity.

Mutagenic Deviation has a warp charge value of 6. If manifested, select one enemy **Infantry** unit within 12" of this psyker. Until the start of your next Psychic phase, when resolving an attack made with a melee weapon by a **Twisted Helix** model from your army against that unit, add 1 to the wound roll.

GENESTEALER CULTS NAME GENERATOR

If you wish to create a name for one of your insidious cultists, you can roll a D66 and consult the table below, or pick a name that inspires you. To roll a D66, simply roll two D6, one after the other – the first represents tens and the second represents digits, giving you a result between 11 and 66.

NEOPHYTE/ACOLYTE NAME GENERATOR TABLE

D66	FORENAME	SURNAME
11	Gannar	Druchmann
12	Dhraz	Kreel
13	Yohrick	Desh
14	Kol	Cavorla
15	Hastun	Krauss
16	Sayben	Gardlinger
21	Hollan	Zorbech
22	Narek	Stennvar
23	Rauss	Varnway
24	Basc	Starn
25	Davon	Baumgart
26	Zask	Drisso
31	Nasser	Sammer
32	Seimon	Helm
33	Jacobiah	Tarnright
34	Skir	Valka
35	Ghaskin	Kelbrech
36	Foyle	Kheiser
41	Kreen	Madrach
42	Judh	Venner
43	Mordecai	Novek
44	Isaak	Svodnor
45	Michon	Black
46	Jerec	Barchus
51	Aldren	Matterzhek
52	Madrax	Onderghast
53	Vyrion	Thrace
54	Hollun	Lhaska
55	Steen	Rezzekh
56	Pike	Carleon
61	Mallick	Drevender
62	Groust	Seifer
63	Eldric	Vreel
64	Yorl	Xyben
65	Xandus	Gorl
66	Crasker	Arnalt